Contents

What Would Colin Do?

101 situations and solutions for every dog groomer

By Colin Taylor

Foreword by Melissa Verplank

Illustrations by Aneta Radomska

*To each and every dog groomer everywhere. And to all
the dogs that make our craft so varied and rewarding.*

Published in Great Britain in 2013 by Grand Union Press Ltd

116 Chamberlayne Road
London NW10 3JP
United Kingdom

www.grandunionpress.co.uk

ISBN 978 0 9575691 0 2

Printed and bound in Great Britain by Stroma Ltd.

A LEGAL DISCLAIMER

Okay. I have to say this to protect myself legally. I have provided a description of the
actions I would take in 101 different situations. Anybody who grooms dogs, or runs a
business that involves dog grooming, might encounter any of these situations.

Some of these are emergency situations. Let's be clear. I am a professional dog groomer. I
am not a qualified vet. If you find yourself in any one of these emergencies, you must take
advice from a vet.

I am, however, allowed to share my experiences. So, when I tell you what I would do, only
take this as a story from another dog groomer. Who happened to be in this situation. This
is what he did. What I did. Or what I would do.

Technically, yes, I provide advice as a professional dog groomer. I have responsibilities
with respect to industry bodies. Certification boards. I provide recommendations
consistent with their guidelines and practices. That's not a problem. I've been teaching for
a long time.

I also deliver my thoughts and opinions about the industry. I share ways to develop a
business. Maintain good customer relationships. Suggest ways you can become successful.

Some of the situations have been amended. To assist the instructional aims of this book.
For dramatic effect. Or because I could get a good joke out of it. Names of dogs, or people
I've worked with, have been changed. Except for some of the real life people whose
names I mention.

I can't guarantee that this book will make you a better dog groomer. A better dog handler.
A better business owner. Or even a better person. Results will vary, as they say.

All I can do is tell my story. Hopefully you will be inspired by it.

Colin Taylor
London, 2013

Acknowledgements

This book might have remained just an idea. Rattling about in my head. A messy outline, scribbled on the back of an envelope. Abandoned in a coffee shop.

But it isn't. It's here. In your hands. And for that, you can blame the following people. But I would like to thank them:

To Melissa Verplank. Who wrote the foreword. Who provided indispensable feedback during the writing. Proof-reading. Editing.

To the very talented Aneta Radomska. Who created such stylish illustrations. I absolutely love them. And I'm sure you will too.

To Gill East. Who taught me. Who is still my inspiration. And friend.

To Dina Perry. Who brought me to the US. And tolerated my getting stuck in the mud. Sort of.

To Julie Harris, Sue Zecco, Lesley Garratt and Janette Bishop. Who all took the time and trouble to preview the text. And send their feedback.

To Coleman Oviatt and Martin Jakubowski in particular. Who pushed me to start this project. And contributed such valuable observations.

To Kristian Maris, my editor. Were it not for his patience, fine-tuning and sense of humour, this book would not have been made a reality.

To my mum and dad. Who always encouraged me to pursue my passion. Thank you. With love.

Last, but not least. My students. On courses. Or in workshops. Thank you for always asking me so many questions.

From the bottom of my heart, I thank you all.

Any mistakes or inconsistencies. Silly jokes impossible to understand. Factual errors. Or plain nonsense that survived the editing. These are my fault alone.

xx Colin
London, 2013

Foreword

Colin Taylor and I have been friends for a very long time. When I first met Colin he was only 19 years old. He had just arrived in America. He could barely work out our monetary system. Putting the correct amount of coins into the soda machine was a challenge for him. Oh…. and that British accent. He was fine as long as he remained calm and cool. You could understand what he was saying. No problem. But get him the least bit excited – there was no understanding what he was saying through that accent!

His compassion for dogs is always at the forefront of *everything* that he does. Put a dog on the table and a pair of shears in Colin's hands - and it was magic. His talent was undeniable. He turned heads and gained respect for those talents wherever he went around the world.

Colin has had a wide variety of job offers. He's taken advantage of many of them. He's had a life full of experience. He's gained knowledge firsthand - at the ground level. As a groomer. As a stylist. As a teacher. As a judge. As a coach. Throughout his career, Colin has always groomed every day pets – just like most of us.

In his book, *What Would Colin Do?* he (or his alter ego sidekick, Precious) tackle everyday questions and concerns. And he's not shy with the questions. Oh no. He tells it like it is – but with a great dose of humor tossed in.

The 101 situations come directly from firsthand experience in the trenches. Sometimes the situations are serious. Sometimes they're awkward. Sometimes it's about money. Or it could be about the dog and other times it's about the customer. But whatever the situation, they are typical scenarios that play out in careers with dogs.

Many times we might second guess ourselves. Did we do the right thing? What should I have done? Or, what will I do? Now you have a book that can guide you through those challenging circumstances!

Colin doesn't pretend that he has all the answers - he doesn't. For almost every situation, there's multiple ways to handle it 'correctly.' It's similar to dog grooming. There's no one correct way to groom any dog - yet there are lots of options.

What Colin does have is a wealth of knowledge and experience under his belt. In his book *What Would Colin Do?* he shares his thoughts, his ideas and his experience with you in a very entertaining way. As I read through the 101 scenarios, I couldn't stop reading - nor could I quit chuckling. This is totally pure Colin Taylor! The information held within the pages is just good solid common sense. And these days, sometimes common sense isn't so easy to come by!

 It is his hope (and Precious's too) that you will be inspired and motivated to do the right thing for the dog, the client and yourself as you face difficult situations in your own career as a professional pet stylist.

Melissa Verplank
Founder & President
~ The Paragon School of Pet Grooming, Inc.
~ White Dog Enterprises, Inc.
~ MelissaVerplank.com
~Whiskers Resort & Pet Spa, Inc.
~ Learn2GroomDogs.com

Who this book is for. And why.

I wrote this book for every dog groomer. Or anybody connected to the dog grooming industry. No matter what level of experience or expertise you may have. You could be starting out. You could be an Old Pro. You might be a young, handsome, modest Pro. Like me. Did I mention 'young'?

Maybe you're a mobile groomer. A dog walker who wants to groom your client's dogs. Perhaps you work in a famous high-end salon. Or just completed your training. You've decided to change career. Open your own shop. Or you're the Managing Director of a chain of dog grooming salons. You might be a newly hired grooming assistant.

Or you're my cousin Jen. And don't know anything about dogs. And picked up this book because my mum ordered you to (Hi Jen!).

This book is for you. Because in this book are more than 100 situations that any one of us could find ourselves in (except Jen of course).

The situation could be anything related to dog grooming. It doesn't have to be a bad thing. Or an emergency. Yes, I look at what I would do if there were an accident in the salon. If a dog had a seizure during grooming.

But I also talk about how I have improved my dog grooming over the years. How my grooming has become more efficient and standardised. How I choose a set of clippers. Or use comb attachments. Riveting stuff, really. Plus I get into some workplace hazards. How to avoid them.

We talk about happy things. Like career development. Christmas bookings. Managing customer relationships. Developing your skills. Your business. Competing.

In a few places, it gets personal. So be warned. I share some of my hang-ups. Jangled nerves. Secret anxieties. Lack of self-confidence.

And how I stay motivated. After all, I'm only human. I have off-days. We all do. But the show must go on. So I share a mental exercise that was taught to me early on. I still use it today.

Of course, my 'solutions' are what 'I' would do. I am not pronouncing gospel. If you're already grooming, you will have come across any number of these. What YOU would do might be better than what I would do. In which case, let me know. I am keen about opening up a dialogue. Getting feedback. Hearing from you.

Introducing Precious

There are two sides to Colin.

One side of Colin is this guy who hates to shave. Or get smartened up for any occasion. He'd much rather crash on his sofa. Listen to Kylie. Or watch crap television. He's mad about X-Factor.

Then, there is this other side. ME. I am Colin's ultra-ego. Not alter-ego. His ULTRA-EGO.

You can call me Precious. I'm snappy. I'm bright. I'm confident. I'm in control. And I have wonderful dress sense. And yes, I'm just a little high maintenance. But all in a good way.

So here's how it works.

Colin and I (his 'ultra' ego) had a chat. He was drinking a cappuccino. I was having an exotic cocktail. It had a little umbrella in it (I love cocktails with little umbrellas).

Colin was talking about all the experiences of his long, long, long grooming career.

We made a list.

Matted dogs. Bleeding nails. Competitions. Making money. Difficult customers.

If you're a groomer, you'll know what I mean.

I told Colin he needed to share these situations – and his solutions - with ALL groomers. They don't need to be the right solutions. Just what he would do.

That way, other groomers don't have to panic if the same thing happens to them. They can just look up *What Would Colin Do?*

Brilliant, right? I'm a genius.

Now, we might not have covered every situation from here to Timbuk-Toblerone. But we've got a lot of them. 101 to be precise.

And I make a bunch of appearances. Sure, Colin can handle most things. But when the grooming gets tough, I get grooming.

I'm the one who shuts down chaos. I block out silly frazzled nerves and worries. I put Colin in a zone of cool cucumber control.

So you'll have me for some of the tougher situations.

But be warned: between Colin and me there is some friendly rivalry. Some humorous banter. It keeps us from getting too serious about ourselves.

Wait. I hear heavy footsteps. It's Colin. Marching over. He wants a word.

COLIN: thanks for indulging this light introduction to 'Precious'. I don't really have a diagnosed split personality. But I do have something in me that sort of kicks in. When things become stressful. It's like an alter-ego. So I have given it a name. I call it Precious. It's just a bit of fun.

This is not to be frivolous, though. There are serious parts to this book. It is designed to be educational.

A lot of what I've written is how I'll talk to my students. It keeps the teaching and the learning fun. For me anyway (lol). Otherwise you just end up with a conventional text-book. Which you might have preferred. But it's not really my style.

Either way, I hope you get something out of it. That you don't find Precious distracting and annoying (she can be irksome). And, as well, that you love the illustrations as much as I do.

Nothing would make me happier than to walk into your salon one day. To see my book. Lying open on a table. Or tucked into your magazine rack in the bathroom. To discover that it's been thoroughly thumbed through. Messy with coffee stains. Marked up with a highlighter. Scribbles and doodles everywhere. Literally falling apart from use.

Just don't draw little horns coming out of my head please. I'm superstitious like that.

xx Colin (and Precious)

Colin's Six Rules

for the Grooming Salon

I have these hanging up in my salon. So I thought I'd share them with you.

1. ALWAYS CLOSE DOORS BEHIND YOU – NEVER LET A DOG ESCAPE

2. NEVER LEAVE A DOG UNATTENDED – EXPECT THE UNEXPECTED

3. ALWAYS OFFER WATER TO DOGS BECAUSE THEY CAN'T ASK YOU

4. NEVER BRUSH OUT A BADLY MATTED DOG BECAUSE IT WILL HURT THE DOG

5. KEEP YOURSELF AND OTHERS AROUND YOU SAFE FROM HARM AND INJURY

6. ALWAYS BE HONEST WITH YOUR CLIENTS. IT WILL BENEFIT YOU, THEM AND THEIR DOG

1. Perfectionism

When I was younger, I was a perfectionist. These were early days in my career. I would watch my colleagues do an immaculate job on their dogs. I'd be frustrated. My dogs didn't look as good.

I would concentrate even more. And get nit-picky about every detail. I was never ready to let the dog leave the salon. Not until it looked perfect. As you can imagine, this slowed me down. It became an impractical way to work.

I was told to speed up. But I struggled. I knew the specific lines I was unhappy with. Where the hair didn't fall as nicely as it should. Where the balance was slightly off.

I was working in a commercial grooming salon. I wasn't grooming for the show-ring. Yet I was putting all this pressure on myself.

Perfectionism is a problem. It slows you down. And this doesn't just apply to grooming dogs. It applies to all manner of things. Which can affect your business. Like choosing an image for your advertising. Selecting a new dryer. Or just plain making a decision about anything.

So how do you stop being a perfectionist? Perfectionism is heavily loaded with self-esteem issues. And that's a whole other minefield. Big books are written on the subject. But not this book.

For our purposes, my advice is this: yes, you need to be good. Yes, you need to work efficiently. These things come the more you groom. So keep grooming. And work on your time.

Unless you're grooming show-dogs full-time, you are most likely working in a commercial salon. Your dogs, therefore, are people's pets. The priorities are different between dogs for show and dogs that are everyday pets.

Instead of trying to groom for the show ring, we should focus instead on achieving the 'acceptable' cut for the everyday dog.

Let's be pragmatic (that's a Precious word but I love it: 'pragmatic'. Sounds like a cool old car. I can see myself, top down, speeding along in my 1957 Chevy Pragmatic... okay, I'm driving off-topic...).

I will often say to students "good is good enough".

Yes, you need to take your time. Yes, you have to make sure the dog looks good. But don't be overly fussy correcting every line or shape. Think about what the customer will see when they come to collect their dog. Put the dog on the floor. Step back. Take a look. Is it acceptable?

If you've done a good job, stop obsessing. Because you need to get onto the next dog.

2. Show Grooming vs. Commercial Grooming

PRECIOUS: Colin has done well in competition. And grooming show dogs. Then he hears it all the time. People telling him that his customers must be thrilled. Because they get HIM to groom THEIR dogs.

His nose starts to twitch. Like he's about to sneeze.

Sure, some of the best SHOW groomers in the world are also full-time PET groomers. Running their own salons. Grooming pet dogs when they're not on the show circuit.

But it's not like they're grooming for show when they're grooming everyday household pets.

Grooming for show requires weeks of advance preparation. The dog isn't just magically turned out in the space of a couple of hours. Colin will be hired by the show dog owner or handler. Practise on the dog. And on the big day, spend hours getting it ready for the show ring.

If the dog places, it will be shown again later in the day. So Colin has to stay put. It's an all-day affair.

Grooming PET dogs is less intense.

We sometimes get customers who bring in a picture. For example, a Lhasa Apso that has just won best in show somewhere. They would like their domestic pet Lhasa Apso to look like the dog in the picture.

And there he is. The Lhasa Apso in the picture. Prancing majestically across the red carpet. A gentle sway in the long silky strands of its beard and skirt and tail. Towards the big, golden trophy.

Uhm, okay. The grooming we provide is based on breed requirements for shows like Westminster and Crufts. But it's not realistic to expect a show standard on an everyday pet.

Yes we can make the dogs look good. Similar to show cuts. But the way we groom will be different.

As for the Lhasa Apso in our salon? He's cute. He has a nice coat. But the owners don't fuss over it like professional show people.

Let's consider the English Cocker Spaniel. For the show ring, it would be stripped, or carded. The furnishings longer and flowing. But styled.

The Cocker pet however? We can achieve a 'stylistically' similar result. But our means of getting there will differ. For example, Colin will use clippers on the body instead of hand-stripping.

The same applies to most Terrier breeds.

When it comes to Poodles, it's a different ball game. The show style is nowhere close to the everyday pet style. And the handlers of show Poodles are likely to be doing the grooming themselves.

Dog groomers who like to compete, however, will learn to groom Poodles for show. It's an exciting part of competing to master a Poodle show cut.

So, you may have to disappoint your customer. The end result will be determined by the coat and the dog itself. Unfortunately, it's not likely their dog will win the prize for Best in Show. But it will still look wonderful.

3. Pre-Grooming Consultation

Before you take a dog into the grooming salon, you have to establish "what we'd like done today."

It's like me going to the barber shop. Make me look like George Clooney, I say. The barber has a rant. That will take him fifteen minutes on top of the normal time. He'll have to charge me extra!

So I tell him not to worry. Maybe next time. But seriously, the pre-grooming consultation is SO important. This is your chance to inspect the dog's coat. To ask the owner the dog's history. I do the following.

I run my fingers through the dog's coat. Usually I can see immediately whether or not the dog is matted. But getting hands-on, I try to detect anything unusual on the skin. Could be a mole. Could be a grass seed. A tick. An abnormal bump. Or a scab from a recent cut.

If I find anything, I'll ask the customer.

I inspect the pads. Look at the condition of the nails. I check the ears. The teeth and gums. The eyes.

If you've done a course, this will have been part of your training. I am checking for anything that needs attention.

I will agree the desired coat length with the customer. What to do with the tail. Face. Ears. Legs.

I'll establish the time it should take.

And I will tell the customer the expected price.

The pre-grooming consultation therefore serves a couple of functions. First, that the dog is fit and healthy for grooming. That we have addressed any medical conditions. Old cuts. Strange bumps. Or behavioural issues.

Second, we manage the customer's expectations. They can leave with an idea of how the dog will look afterwards. How long the grooming will take. How much it will cost.

IF you don't cover these things, you are unprepared.

Don't have the dog's history? What if he suddenly turns on you? And leaves a nasty bite?

Didn't know the dog had a meaty scab from a recent cut on its hind leg? Now you have a dog in the bath bleeding. With an open wound. And the customer might think it's your fault.

Didn't know the dog was badly matted? The customer asked you to keep it long. So if you clip off, it's going to be a shock. This is poor service. You could have told them what to expect.

I make a number of references through the book to the pre-grooming consultation. It doesn't have to be a strict interrogation or anything. It only needs to take a couple of minutes. It should be jolly and pleasant.

Customers always appreciate it when you show real, hands-on interest in their dog. It reassures them that their dog is in capable hands. Plus we all like to have our expectations managed. It's a communication thing. I insist on it.

4. Prepping

A friend of mine wants to open his own restaurant one day. I can hardly wait. So he's got a job working for a famous chef. Right now, he's 'prepping'. Which means he does all the chopping. The slicing and dicing. Bowl after bowl of fresh-cut mushrooms. Potatoes. Tomatoes. Chicken. Pork. Beef.

He gets all these ingredients ready so the chef doesn't have to lose time doing it herself. She can march into the kitchen like a celebrity. Whip it all together in a saucepan. Create a culinary masterpiece.

There is a similar pecking order in dog grooming. We start with the prepping. Which is to get the dog ready for grooming.

Depending on where you work, a junior groomer may prep the dog first. The senior dog groomer – or celebrity stylist – can march into the salon. Scissor and style the dog. Create a masterpiece.

Or, in most cases, we groom the dogs ourselves from start to finish. Including the prepping.

With prepping, I do the following:

* Inspect the pads and clip or trim in-between
* clip the nails
* inspect the ears. Pluck or trim the dead hair if necessary. Clean the ears
* clip the hygiene area
* check the anal glands. If they need expressing I will do this first thing after I get them into the bath
* if I'm going to take the dog short, I will clip the coat. Just a basic clip at this point, nothing perfect. I call it 'roughing in'. The coat might be dirty.

But I will save time by going short now. Instead of having to wash and dry the longer coat
* the dog then goes into the bath
* two vigorous warm water baths. Followed by a thorough, squeaky-clean rinse
* blow-dry followed by brushing and combing, before styling

Some groomers might do the nails in the final stages of grooming. But if you accidentally cut a quick, you could get a bloody nail. So if you do the nails at the start, a cut quick will have a chance to heal. By the time the customer is ready to collect their dog, the nail will have stopped bleeding. I have a section later on about accidentally cutting the quick.

The purpose of prepping is to ready the dog for grooming. To an ideal state. The stylist can then just go to work with their clippers or scissors. Not having to worry about whether or not the ears still need doing. Or the nails still need clipping.

We are working to a 'method'. An agreed and understood program that all grooming in my salon follows. It makes sure we haven't forgotten something. And improves our efficiency.

5. Treating the Ears

Regular grooming isn't simply about providing dogs a haircut. It's part of maintaining overall health and well-being. We call this 'preventative care'.

A standard feature of grooming, like clipping nails, is treating the dog's ears. It involves cleaning the ears and plucking the dead hair from inside the ear canal.

Not all breeds grow hair inside their ears. Most gun dogs and your double-coated breeds for example. So don't be shocked if you look inside and can't see any hair that needs plucking.

The hair to be plucked is 'dead' hair or hair that comes loose easily. If you have to tug hard, it will hurt. Plucking should never be painful.

I start by sprinkling some ear powder lightly onto the hair inside the ear. This will help my fingers and thumb to get a dry, firm hold. I make sure not to put too much powder in the ear. This can cause build-up. And may interfere with the ear's own natural cleaning and removal of foreign objects.

I don't dig too deep into the ear canal. I only pluck the dead hair that I can see easily.

Like our own ears, dog's ears are a sensitive part of the anatomy. They need to be handled carefully. Carelessness could lead to infection and potential damage. Whether that's hearing loss. Problems to do with balance. Or worse.

Some groomers prefer to use forceps or tweezers. If you use forceps, be careful not to pinch the dog's skin. This may cause the dog to jump suddenly. Which could lead to an accident.

Afterwards, I clean the dog's ears with a cleaning solution and cotton swabs. This gets rid of built-up ear wax and any remaining powder. It also gives the ear a fresh smell.

If I have a dog that hates having his ears handled, I will try to get a little bit done at a time. I'll ask the owner to come back in a few days. And I'll try again. If the dog is totally uncooperative, I'll refer the owner to the vet instead.

I see a lot of dogs with ear infection. The ear reeks. The inside of the ear may have a dark, greasy build-up. The dog will yelp in pain when his ear is handled.

Often the infection is chronic and recurring. The owners have been in and out of the vet. They've tried everything. Expensive ear drops. Canker powder. Regular grooming. In these cases, the dogs may benefit from trimming the hair. Instead of plucking.

A friend has tried this recently with her Standard Poodle. She uses a mini-clipper on the shortest setting. Removes the bulk of the hair. Then swabs the ear with a cleanser and cotton swabs.

Guess what. No more on-going ear infections. She started practising this in her own salon. With dramatic results. So she told two friends. And they followed the same advice in their salons. Again. Dramatic results.

So I'm now doing this for the dogs I see with recurring ear infection.

6. Cutting Nails

Trimming a dog's nails often makes new groomers a little nervous. That's because we have to face the risk of cutting the quick. Which can be painful for the dog. And can create a bloody mess.

When you look at the diagram of a nail, you will see that the hard shell of the nail covers a blood vessel. This blood vessel is called the 'quick'. When we take a nail too short - any groomer with experience will have done this by accident – it means we have hit the blood vessel. Which means the nail will bleed. Some breeds have nails that are clear. It's easy to see the pink outline of the quick inside the nail. Trim the nail at a point beyond the quick. No problem.

Other breeds have nails that are black. It's impossible to see the quick. Dog's nails normally curve. It's generally safe to cut just before where the nail starts to bend. It's also helpful to look into the nail tip. Cut a little at a time. Look for a white circle in the centre of the nail. This will indicate that you are getting close to the quick.

I normally clip a dog's nails during prepping. That way, if there is a bleeding nail, I'll have the duration of the grooming for any bleeding to stop. When a nail bleeds, I apply Quick Stop or other coagulant in powder form.

I also always tell my customer. It's minor. I have treated it. There shouldn't be any problems. And they shouldn't freak out if they spot some blood droplets later at home.

If the owner is worried, I explain that it's a bit like nicking yourself shaving. You don't need to rush to the Emergency department. Just apply a small rip of tissue paper to stop the bleeding. And it's fine. Likewise, the owner doesn't need to rush to the vet.

The only exception to this – and it's rare – is if the dog has blood clotting disease. Tell the customer to keep an eye on the quick. If it continues to bleed after a few hours, they should see the vet.

You will sometimes meet a dog with neglected nails. The nail has grown full circle and is now sticking into the pad of the dog's paw. It happens often with the dew claw. I tell the customer they have a couple of options.

If the nail is physically ingrown, the safest option is the vet. Who may suggest surgery. Which may require putting the dog under general anaesthetic. The vet will make sure everything is done by the book. An open wound on the foot is exposed to the elements. Dogs travel anywhere and everywhere on their feet.

The other option is that I take care of it. I've treated an ingrown nail hundreds of times without incident. I cut the nail at the centre of the circle. If it's physically ingrown, I pull the nail remnant out. There may be some blood. So I'll do this gently.

I treat the pad with alcohol-free iodine to make sure it is properly sterilised. I'll ask the customer to keep a close eye to prevent any possible infection.

7. Cleaning Teeth

Although I will check a dog's teeth and gums during the pre-grooming consultation, that's as far as it goes. I don't provide teeth cleaning.

Some salons offer teeth cleaning as routine within a Full Groom. What they often mean is a squirt of some anti-bacterial gel into the mouth. The groomer might use her finger or a toothbrush to slide the gel over the teeth and gums.

I think it's misleading to describe this as teeth cleaning. 'Breath freshening' or 'mouthwash' is probably more appropriate.

For the most part, dogs don't like anybody touching their teeth. They fidget. You struggle to hold them. And sometimes they bite. That's a problem.

Personally, I'm not convinced it's worth the trouble.

You might have come across 'ultra-sonic tooth cleaning.' There are trained practitioners who can provide this service. Often they are dog groomers. Providing it from their own salons.

I have seen the results. It looks good. But I think of this as a specialist service. To be offered by trained professionals. If that's you, it could be a good little add-on to a grooming business.

So I am totally open-minded about it. And see it as a good step in preventative care.

Vets, however, might be less enthusiastic. They might think of it as a cosmetic treatment, rather than a proper teeth cleaning. That's because it cannot be as thorough as scraping built-up plaque and hard tartar from the teeth of a sedated dog. Especially around the gum line.

If I notice a dog with teeth and gum problems, I'll tell the customer to go to the vet. Generally though, for dogs with normal healthy teeth and gums, I recommend various supplements. As preventative care. Some of these have shown good results preventing or eliminating the build-up of plaque and tartar.

Rawhide and other chews are also good at scraping off soft plaque. And playing with rope is helpful. The dog sinks its teeth into the rope, which rubs off the soft plaque.

You can consider investing the time and money in ultra-sonic tooth cleaning. Make it a unique selling proposition for your business. But I suggest you do your homework. Make sure the figures stack up correctly (profitably).

8. Anal Glands

PRECIOUS: Luck of the draw. And guess what?! It's me, Precious. Talking to you about anal glands. Lovely. Thanks Colin.

Well, there is no easy way around it. Let's get to the bottom of this sticky issue.

Ever notice that foul fish-like odour coming from a dog's back-end? Or notice the dog scooting along the floor on his hind quarters? Perhaps nipping at his butt?

These are common signs that the dog may need its anal glands (or anal sacs) expressed. Squeezed. So that the built up fluid is emptied.

In a lot of dogs, the procedure is never necessary. That's because it's taken care of naturally every time they poo. You'll notice this among your own dogs. The occasional run of fluid that comes out when they poo. That's the anal glands releasing built-up fluid naturally.

In some dogs this isn't always the case. Instead, fluid collects in the anal sacs. The help of a 'friend' is needed to release the build-up.

Now, is this a job for a dog groomer, or the vet? Or maybe even for the dog owner themselves?

A generation ago, salons would express anal glands routinely. Many still do. Recently though, some salons are less ready to do it. Instead, they recommend taking the dog to the vet.

If done incorrectly, it could lead to ruptured anal glands. And that means on-going problems for the rest of the dog's life. Some salons aren't happy to take that risk.

Or you'll notice more salons asking their customers to sign a waiver. They don't want to be held legally responsible if something goes wrong.

Anal glands can become 'impacted' (hardened up so that, a bit like constipation, the fluids are unable to be expressed easily). Trying to express impacted glands increases the risk of accidental rupture. So you need to know when NOT to express. Refer the owner to the vet instead.

You might think this is all a bunch of nonsense. A waiver? For anal glands? What next? You've done it a million times. Never had any problems. You wonder what all the fuss is about.

And I'd agree. But we live in litigious times. Some salon owners just find it easier to hand the customer a waiver. Or send them to the vet.

When I groom, I check if the anal glands need expressing. If yes, then I'll do it. But I don't do it as a matter of routine.

I express the glands in the bath, before I start the shampoo treatment. I lift the tail. I check if the anus is protruding (like puckered up lips ready for a kiss - although it's just wrong to use that analogy).

If so, then I know that the dog's anal glands MIGHT need expressing. I put my thumb and third finger on either side of the lower part of the anus. If I feel that it is hardened – but not too hard - then I know the glands need expressing.

You'll want to wear surgical gloves for this, by the way.

I then push slowly inwards. Until I feel my thumb and finger behind each gland. I squeeze my thumb and finger together slightly. Then draw towards myself.

You don't want your face staring into the dog's bum at this point. Sometimes the anal fluid will squirt straight out like a water pistol. I have yet to see a video of this on YouTube. But I'm sure it's a matter of time.

It all depends on the pressure of the build-up. So be careful. It may also just ooze out with a thick runny texture.

Yep, it's stinky and smelly.

Repeat the gentle squeezing until the anus stops secreting.

IF the dog yelps at any point during this process, stop immediately. Tell the owner that you tried. They'll need to see the vet instead. It may be more than just built-up fluid. It could be a sharp food object in one of the glands. Or a blockage of some sort.

Leave this to the vet. You can't risk creating a worse situation.

Job done. Make sure to rinse all the anal juice away. And you can get started with your shampoo.

I've described above the way that I do it. But a vet may also do it by inserting a finger into the rectum.

This is not an approach I recommend for an everyday dog groomer. Not unless you really know what you're doing. Or you've got the experience as a vet or vet nurse yourself.

Some dog owners might ask you if it's something they can do themselves at home. I will ask them to take advice from their vet. You don't want to get mixed up with a dog owner's DIY. If something goes wrong, the finger will be pointed at you. Plus you'll annoy the vet for interfering. So stay neutral on this.

Since we're talking about the dog's anus, you might sometimes see worms. Don't freak out. It happens. It looks really gross. But I just feel sorry for the poor dog. No wonder he's scooting his butt along the floor.

Be extremely careful that the worms don't get anywhere in your salon. The risk is that they slip out of the dog's anus. And could be ingested by another dog.

So you'll want to keep that dog separate. Perhaps in a crate or holding area after it's been groomed. Ask the customer to collect their dog as soon as possible. Tell them what you saw. In graphic detail. This will motivate them to make sure the dog is immediately wormed.

And be nice to the dog for the time he is still with you. Don't make him feel like a complete social outcast just because the poor fella's got worms.

9. Fleas

For the record: I hate fleas. Yes, I know we must value all God's creatures. But even God must make an exception for fleas. These terrible parasites have to be dealt with forcefully and swiftly.

Over the last few years, the number of dogs I have seen with fleas has certainly declined compared to, say, a generation ago. That's because the flea preventative treatments have been really effective. A little more recently though it seems the normal brands aren't strong enough. So the manufacturers have had to come up with yet stronger treatments.

Nine times out of ten we spot a flea too late. The dog is already inside our salon. And that's a problem. I'll need to treat the dog with a flea shampoo. If the dog has mingled with other dogs in the salon I may need to provide a flea shampoo for them as well. I can't take the risk. A dog that came into my salon WITHOUT fleas should never go home WITH fleas.

On top of all that, I may have to treat the salon with a pesticide. Like a fumigating flea bomb.

When bathing a dog with fleas, don't be alarmed if you see the water running red. It's not blood. You haven't done anything wrong.

The RED comes from the flea faeces. How cool is that? Okay, not cool.

Try the following. You know those specks that look like pepper next to the dog's skin? That's flea faeces. Take one of these specks. Put it on a piece of moist paper towel. Watch what happens. These specks (the faeces) leave a rusty red mark. Which explains the water running red.

After the grooming, you'll have to tell the customer. But tell the customer discreetly and sensitively. Some customers just might take it as an insult. It's not. It's probably just bad luck. And it's really rather common.

If you have a licence to sell flea preventative treatments, this is a good opportunity. Otherwise, recommend a visit to the vet for the stronger variety. You can also provide a special flea shampoo. But this is only a short term fix that is a reaction to a problem. The buzz word these days is 'prevention'. This helps owners avoid flea problems in the first place.

10. Ticks & Tricks

Ticks are found in tall grassy or wooded areas. They are prevalent in summer when the weather is warm. You'll often see ticks on a dog that is allowed to run off-lead. Or has spent time in the country just being a dog.

Ticks are a problem and are tricky to remove.

Some important things to be aware of:

* ticks can carry a number of serious diseases. They need to be removed.

* ticks hook themselves onto the dog's skin with their front pincers.

* ticks can be difficult to see in a dog's coat or on the skin. The tick looks like a small wart. Or a crust-like bump on the skin, with a hard round shell.

* when you remove a tick, make sure it IS a tick. Not a wart.

If we fail to find the tick during the pre-grooming consultation, it's likely we'll discover them during bathing and drying.

I will wait until the dog is dried before removing the tick. I'll be careful not to touch it or remove it accidentally. And I'll be on the lookout for other ticks. Often when I come across one, there are others.

I will take a small dish. Something like a jar top is ideal. This is where I will place the tick as soon as I remove it from the skin. Then I get some paper towel.

You may have been told to apply rubbing alcohol directly onto the tick. But this can actually cause the tick to tighten up. Cause it to deposit more infection into the dog. Or make the tick harder to remove.

With the paper towel between my thumb and index finger, I grab hold of the tick's body. I don't make skin contact.

I pinch my thumb and index finger together and take hold of the tick at the base. I don't take hold at the point where it's digging into the skin. This risks breaking the tick off, leaving some of it behind, still attached.

I pull on the tick in an upward motion away from the skin. Not to the side. I just pull straight out. It's important to remove all of the tick.

I place it in the jar top. The tick will still be alive and I may see its legs moving. I won't allow it to escape from the jar top. I'll need to kill it.

I do this by putting the tick in a jar of rubbing alcohol. Or I'll freeze the tick to kill it. Either way, I make sure it is dead before disposing of it. With apologies to Buddha.

This process of removing the tick will leave a small sore area on the dog's skin. I will treat the area with an anti-septic spray or cream. And I always tell the owner to keep an eye on the sore area.

There is room for error in my method.

IF you are new to grooming, the better option may be to use an O'Tom tick remover. These never leave the heads in. And many of my respected colleagues absolutely swear by them.

11. Smelly Dog

PRECIOUS: It's a Sunday morning. My head aches. The sun annoys me. I'm drinking a glass of tomato juice. With Worcestershire sauce. A bit of Tabasco. There's a floral celery stick in my glass.

And all I can think of is a beagle named Charlie.

It's the tomato juice.

I was merrily enjoying my Saturday in the salon. This is back in the days when Colin and I lived in the US. I just finished scissoring a Bischon. I was ready to put my tools away. And clean up. I had a great evening planned. First the bowling lanes with the girls. Then Lola's for 'Crantinis'. And a bit of dancing.

Then Charlie happened. Charlie was the neighbour's dog. A beagle. Adventurous. Free-spirited. But unlucky. Especially when it came to skunks. Charlie got sprayed.

He needed a bath. Not the hypo-allergenic Oatmeal bath. Or the ultra-mild 'essence of Zanzibar'. He needed a serious treatment.

It's a cliché. We see it in the movies. Or laugh about it in the comics. A dog gets sprayed by a skunk. The solution is a bath in tomato juice. Endless tins of tomato juice.

There are specialist shampoos on the market designed to deal with skunk spray. We normally kept an emergency ration in the salon. But I couldn't find any. I had also heard of a homemade remedy. Baking powder, hydrogen peroxide and washing-up liquid. But we went for tomato juice. And bought a few big tins from the shop next door.

Skunk spray is the liquid that the skunk stores in its anal sacs. The skunk uses it defensively. The texture is oily and heavy. So when you wash it off, try not to spread the spray elsewhere onto the body. Just rinse and wash it off the affected area.

It's the odour that gets you. It's a thick terrible, nauseating smell. Like horrible rotten eggs. Mixed with burning roof tar. The odour is persistent. Washing with tin after tin of tomato juice neutralises the odour. There might still have been a faint whiff of skunk on Charlie for a few days. But he came out of this encounter generally okay.

Charlie had been struck on his left hindquarters. He was lucky not to get any into his nose or eyes. That could have been irritating or painful for him. And may have required the intervention of a vet. It also takes that much longer for the skunk odour to fade.

As for the salon, we were not so lucky.

I burned incense for days. Went through a dozen canisters of air freshener. I don't like a smelly salon. And skunk is really smelly.

If you don't live in an area affected by skunks, you're still likely to get the occasional smelly dog. They like to roll in stuff. In the UK, dogs often roll in fox poo. The owners can't bear to wash the dog themselves. So they'll take it to the grooming salon.

The shampoos we use in the salon will take care of fox poo. But I'll usually give the dog a couple of extra treatments. Fox poo is unpleasant. But nowhere as bad as that skunk spray. I can still smell it. Years later. And thousands of miles away.

12. Drying Cabinets & Crates

Personally, I prefer to hand-dry rather than use crates (cages) or cabinets. With hand-drying, I get that much closer to the dog. The force of the blaster or dryer pushes the hair away from the dog's skin. I am always checking that the skin looks healthy.

Also, I am able to take my comb or brush through the dog's coat. With hand-drying, I can prepare the coat for scissoring and styling. The process is, literally, more hands-on.

The drawback? Hand-drying takes more time. So a lot of salons dry with crates. Or use cabinet dryers. It's faster. While the dog is in the crate, the groomer can start prepping the next dog. But there is a risk.

If left unattended - or forgotten - a dog could over-heat. The consequences could be serious. Maybe even fatal.

For this reason, some salons won't take the risk. They'll promote the fact that they hand-dry. That they don't use crates or cabinets.

Some dog owners may even ask. They will want their dog dried by hand. To be reassured there is no risk.

Let's be 'open-minded' about this. You might work at a salon that insists on crate drying. You don't have much choice. Your boss says so.

Drying by crate or cabinet has its advantages. Not just in terms of time-saving. But because the drying is so thorough. And that helps our scissoring.

As for risk, there are risks everywhere in the salon.

We take scissors to dogs. Dogs can be unpredictable. They might move suddenly.

Dogs are secured to a table. They must be constantly supervised. But sometimes we turn our backs to them.

The bathtub and floor can get wet. Slippery. Dangerous.

We go in and out of doors through which dogs can escape.

In everything we do, we have to be risk aware. And risk averse. Vigilant about safety in our working environment.

This applies to crate and cabinet drying. Make sure the dog is never left unattended. If you're using a crate, make sure the metal bars don't get hot to touch. If you're using a cabinet, always set the timer to go off early. So that you can check on the drying progress.

I have worked with crate drying and cabinets. But I've always been cautious. So I will start with hand-drying. Until the coat is 'nearly' dry. Then I'll put the dog in the crate for a SHORT period. Until the coat is thoroughly dry.

It's practical. Time-efficient. And I appreciate the thoroughly dry coat when I'm scissoring. But like I said, my preferred method is to hand-dry completely.

13. Structure of a Dog

Trying to understand a dog's structure may sound medical. More the responsibility of a vet. But it's important for groomers to know structure. I'm not saying you need to know every bone in a dog's body. Rather, having a good understanding of dog anatomy will help your grooming.

Being comfortable with basic canine structure - using a common vocabulary - promotes better communication between groomers. Between more experienced groomers, and their assistants. Between teachers and students.

Perhaps you run a salon and you've hired an assistant or other groomer to help you. You might know the 'vocab'. But do the people working with you?

I may tell you to clip from the Occiput to the base of the tail. Or clip down the back leg and stop just above the hock bone. You should know what I mean. It's about working more efficiently.

Knowing a dog's structure will also improve the technical side of your grooming. You'll be able to follow the natural lines - the way in which the coat hangs from the dog's skeletal structure - and achieve a better result.

I encourage you to practise this with fellow groomers or your staff. Find a generic diagram or outline of a dog. Print it off and put an X on the basic structure points. You could even print a larger image and post it on the wall in your salon. If you have to instruct a certain style and you use basic structure, they will understand.

Make sure you cover the following points:

- Stop
- Occiput
- Layback of shoulders
- Breast bone
- Pastern
- Stopper Pad
- Elbow
- Top Line
- Pelvis
- Tuck Up
- Stifle
- Hock

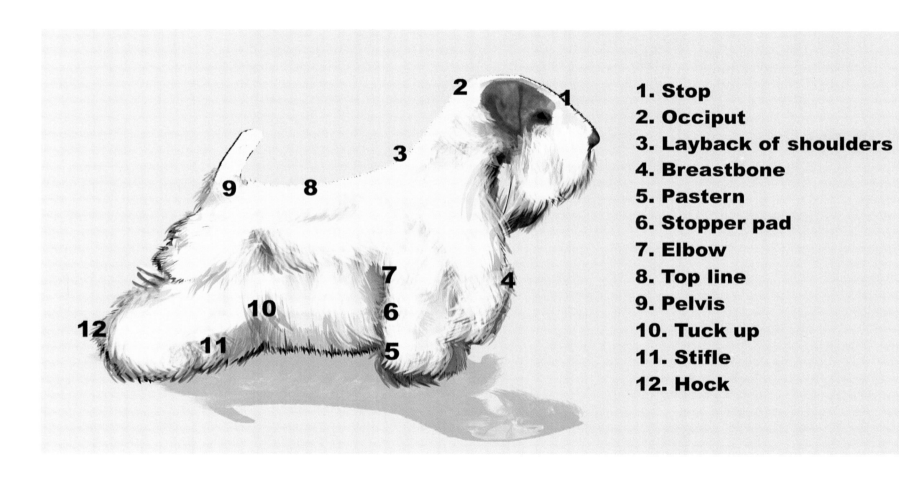

1. Stop
2. Occiput
3. Layback of shoulders
4. Breastbone
5. Pastern
6. Stopper pad
7. Elbow
8. Top line
9. Pelvis
10. Tuck up
11. Stifle
12. Hock

14. Balance

Do you know how some people just 'have it' and others don't?

Knowing how to achieve balance in a dog you're grooming is one of those things.

If you're not a natural, don't despair. You can learn balance. You can train your eye to see balance.

So what do I mean by 'balance'?

Balance comes from a dog's structure. It is three dimensional. It requires symmetry. And correct proportion.

Across the dog's four legs we have to make sure that the cut is even. That the cut is consistent between the two sides of the dog. This is symmetry. Along with this, we need to make sure the head, and the style we are giving the head, along with the tail, are proportional to the rest of the dog.

The starting point for balance is the dog's skeletal structure.

I think of the dog's structure like a blank canvas. The haircut I provide is my interpretation of the breed standard. But following the structure helps me achieve a balanced result. The aim is to carry the flow of the dog's natural structure into your styling.

Provided, of course, that the dog has correct structure to begin with. If it doesn't, then you'll have to leave more hair in some areas. And take more off in others.

This can all get very complicated. I occasionally still find myself struggling to achieve balance correctly on a dog. When that happens, I put the dog on the floor and walk a few feet away so that I can get a good perspective. If I am failing to get part of my styling synchronised with the rest of the dog, I'll be able to see it.

I notice when I'm slightly off if my eye isn't drawn to the centre of the dog. The focal point. If my eye is drawn elsewhere, then my balance is off.

Some of us get it right away. Others of us will have to work a little harder to achieve balance.

For our purposes, this is something not to get too fussy about. You could spend a day trying to perfect the balance of a dog. You'll find yourself taking a little off here or there. But then suddenly that doesn't look quite right. So you keep at it. Trying to perfect it.

Resist this. Good is good enough.

15. Danger Areas When Grooming

It's worth refreshing yourself with a diagram of the dog's anatomy for this. All areas of the dog are at risk of getting cut. But there are some known, identified areas of the dog that I – and others – call 'danger areas'. That's because, nine times out of ten, when a dog has been cut or nicked, it's in one of these areas.

These parts of the body are where the skin looks and feels a lot thinner. As well as those parts of the body not easily visible to the eye when grooming:

- Dewlap or throat
- Armpit
- Tuck up
- Just above the hock bone
- Edges of ears and inside the ear
- Loosely hanging dew claws

To reduce the risk of cutting or nicking the dog when scissoring or trimming, you can do a couple of things. First, kind of obvious, but: know these areas and make sure you pay extra special close attention. Second, move your tools in a new direction.

By 'new direction' I mean 'work away from' the area, rather than 'into' the area. Imagine using your scissors as though cutting away from the body. Into thin air / empty space.

In the dewlap / throat area, watch for the folds of skin. I will pull the skin to make it flat when I'm scissoring this area.

I also recommend you use a tighter toothed blade, such as a 10 or 15 blade. This will minimise the risk of catching the skin between the teeth of the blade.

In general, always minimise the number of distractions around you. Stay focused. But especially pay close attention to these so-called 'danger areas'.

16. Method in Our Madness

Robert De Niro is a 'Method' actor. Which means he's completely 'in character' when he's making a movie. Even when he's not on set. He could be at the catering van. Munching on a cheese sandwich. And he'd still be in character. He would be that guy who's about to punch out your lights. Break your knee caps.

I like to think of myself as a Method Groomer. Like De Niro, I totally commit to the role. Without the punch-ups. I get into 'the zone' when I'm in the salon. And I follow a 'method'.

Let me explain. I will ask a student to style a dog. And then I'll watch as the student starts on the sides. Changes her mind. Moves to another part of the body. Missed a bit here or there. Goes back.

There is no method. No logical step-by-step, section-by-section approach.

So then I take over. I tell the student about Robert De Niro. I tell her to be a Method Groomer.

When I dry a dog my method is: Back. Middle. Front. Head. Tail.

Which means I start drying at the dog's hind-quarters. And work my way up. Making sure each section is dry before moving onto the next.

Then I'll dry the head. And finish with the tail.

When I style the dog, there is a variation.

I start with the rear assembly. I create nice parallel lines between the rear legs.

Then I go to the front assembly. And create nice parallel lines between the front legs.

Then I focus on the middle of the dog. Bringing my styling into correct proportion with the rear and the front.

Then the head.

Finally, the tail.

I'll stand back. Take a look. Make sure my eyes are drawn to the centre of the dog. Make any corrections. And end up with a nice finish. I might not get an Academy Award. But the customer will be pleased.

17. Round Feet & Cups of Tea

My reward after a long day is a big cup of tea. And some biscuits. Especially the shortbread ones with chocolate and a sticky layer of caramel. Sigh.

But, as Precious likes to point out, I always leave a little trail of tea puddles across the floor.

"Why don't you use a saucer you clumsy gorilla," she shouts.

"Because I'm not posh," I shout back. "And a saucer under this giant mug would look just plain silly."

Maybe one day I'll use a saucer. When I'm retired. In the sitting room watching Downton Abbey. Wearing my favourite pashmina. Admiring my collection of little porcelain Bedlington Terriers on the mantelpiece.

So, where am I going with this? I am, of course, talking about creating a nice round foot on a dog.

When I am teaching how to scissor a round foot, I always refer to a cup saucer. It is flat at the bottom (the pad area of the foot). Then it lifts at the edges (where the hair starts to lift from the pad upwards). This is called a convex shape. But I never remember the difference between convex and concave. So I just think of a saucer.

The pads will have been clipped out during prepping. But I double-check. If they need a little more work, I'll do that with my trimmer.

I'm happy with the pads. So I begin by combing the hair down on the foot in its natural state. Then I start scissoring. I don't use my best scissors because I don't accidentally want to catch a nail. And risk ruining them. I slant my scissors slightly so that I'm cutting from underneath the foot. This creates a bevelled edge.

It's always best to start your cut at the front of the foot. This way all you have to do is bring the sides in to match the front. A lot of groomers will start at the sides. But then end up with a more pointed looking foot. You don't want this. Unless you're trying to create a hare foot. Which would be appropriate, for example, for a Bedlington Terrier.

Getting back to that saucer. In case you didn't quite understand. Take an old saucer (not from your mum's finest set). With a washable felt marker, draw the pads of a dog's foot in the centre. Can you see what I mean? It can make more sense if you look at it this way.

18. Scissoring the Front Legs

You've achieved a nice round foot. The next step is a scissored cylinder leg.

Stand your dog on all fours. Look at the legs. You are aiming to achieve parallel lines on the two front legs. The lines may go in slightly at the elbow, or pastern. But that's okay.

The lines start from the bevel you have created on the foot.

When I demonstrate to a student, I make sure the dog's leg is standing naturally on the table. But sometimes I lift the leg off the table. To make the scissoring easier. So I have to hold the foot in a particular position. As though it were standing naturally.

For the front legs, I am scissoring to create a column.

I once got a good tip from a Brazilian groomer friend. Get some paint rollers. The really soft ones that you can also take a grooming brush to. Brush the material on the paint rollers. Then practise scissoring to create a nice columned leg.

Don't use good scissors for this. The material on the rollers will dull them. And don't try this on used paint rollers. It gets really messy. Colourful. But messy.

Once you've mastered scissoring the paint rollers, try it on the dogs. And if you can do it on a Cockerpoo, then you can do it on any breed. Although breeds are different, there is a lot of similarity in how the hair is cut. Create your shape first. Then your finish.

19. Scissoring the Rear Legs

Regardless of dog breed, rear legs are generally shaped the same. Not in terms of hair style. But in the bone structure.

It's easy for us to over-think or complicate things. We assume that a rear leg on an Airedale is different from a Poodle that has been scissored all over.

Yes, the end result looks different. But the way you get there is very similar.

Think about where you go short on the leg. And where you would leave it longer.

We leave areas longer to create style. These areas are the stifle and the hock. This is also where the angulation curves outward from the body.

Where the angulation curves inward would normally be where we take it shorter.

By appreciating the dog's shape more, we will achieve the breed profile. Years ago I would groom a dog and scissor it to perfection. But with almost zero angulation on the dog.

With experience, I gained confidence. I started to understand what I was trying to achieve. I was learning to appreciate the shape. Achieving the breed profile would just come naturally.

These days we don't have to rely just on scissors for a nice finish. That's because snap-on combs (comb attachments) help us get the desired finish. And in much better time.

Basically, don't over-think it. Look at pictures of breed standards. Instead of looking at the difference in breeds, look at what they have in common. Some dogs are small, others are big. Some are long in the body, others short. Whatever the size or purpose of the dog, they all have the same structural shape. Learn to scissor or clip instinctively with the structure and you'll achieve the correct finish.

20. Poodle Feet When the Poodle Hates It

PRECIOUS: I am superb at Poodle feet. And I love the look.

But there's something I have to admit. Some Poodles are a darned struggle.

Not only for me. A lot of times I'll visit a salon. Poodle on the table. Time for the feet. And the Poodle isn't having any of it. It's jumping about. Squirming. Making a racket. Those clippers aren't getting anywhere near my ankles!

I see the groomer. Face getting red. Trying to hold onto the paw. The Poodle pulling away. Over and over it goes.

Time is lost. The Poodle is stressed. The groomer is beat. And the feet look terrible.

If that's the outcome, it's time to ask. Is it really worth it? Does the Poodle really need Poodle feet?

You'll have to be up-front with your customer about this. Let them know that their Poodle hates the clippers. That it really struggles. Gets stressed out.

It's not just bad for the Poodle. It stresses out the other dogs. Which impacts the whole working atmosphere in the salon.

But there is hope. An option. How about a simple, round, scissored foot? This would be in the dog's best interest. And still look lovely.

Sure, it isn't textbook Poodle cut. But we have to do what's in the best interest of the dog.

The customer might be sceptical. So, put on your little diplomacy hat. Ask the customer if you can demonstrate. Put the Poodle on the table. Take the clippers to the feet. Let them see what happens.

Personally, I wouldn't like to see my Poodle get stressed. A puppy might get alarmed initially by having its feet shaved. But, over time, it will get used to it.

It's the adult dog I worry about.

Can't teach an old dog new tricks? Well, in the case of Poodle feet, this might be right. It's not worth your aggravation. Not worth stressing the dog out. Not if the acceptable option is a round, scissored foot.

21. Matted Dogs

In a perfect world, owners would bring their dogs to our salons tangle-free. No knots. No matting. But this is far from a perfect world. I still get regulars who come in with their matted dog. They'll ask me to brush out instead of clipping off.

There are three reasons why I think this happens:

1. They prefer their dog to look more breed-specific. Or cute. So they'd like to keep the hair longer.

2. They simply don't understand that de-matting is painful. Or that it is time-consuming. Difficult. And carries increased risk of cutting the dog's skin.

3. They don't appreciate the importance of keeping on top of the grooming themselves.

The owner isn't a groomer. They don't necessarily get it. They need to be educated.

If they show up with a matted dog, this is my opportunity. And what better than to show them with a real life example? Their own dog.

You can imagine me in the salon. Happily playing Angry Birds on my iPad. Waiting for the next customer to arrive.

Madame Marvellous comes through the door. With Fifi. Her Yorkshire Terrier.

Madame Marvellous adores Fifi. She carries her in a handbag. Buys her cashmere jumpers. Diamante collars. Unfortunately, she is a bit lazy with the brushing. And now her little Yorkie is matted.

She can't imagine her darling doggie shaved.

"Can't you just brush her out," she asks me.

Now comes the lesson. I explain that Fifi has a silky coat that requires regular brushing. Perhaps a good brush every second day. It doesn't have to take long. She is a small dog, after all. Ten minutes might be all that is necessary. And her dog will love it because she gets to be the centre of attention.

I take a small slicker brush and apply it to Fifi's coat. I demonstrate on a section that doesn't have any knots in it. I take the brush close to the skin. But not onto the skin. I pull it through the hair. All the tiny pins glide smoothly through the long silky strands.

Madame M is impressed. But I can see she's starting to feel guilty.

I move the brush over to a clump of knotted, twisted hair. She stops me. She can see that the brush won't pull through the hair. She's right. I might get it through eventually. But it would pull so badly on the skin. The pain would be terrible.

I put the brush down.

"Do you see how the hair has formed this really tight, twisting tangle," I ask.

"This is really bad for Fifi's skin. The hair is actually pulling. Causing microscopic little cuts in the surface."

"This is painful. On top of that, there are all kinds of parasites and bacteria that like to harbour inside dense matted hair. There is risk of infection."

Madame M is starting to feel unwell. She begs me to shave Fifi. She promises to stay on top of the brushing.

Often you'll have dogs that come to you with a few mats hidden in the coat. You can clip these out but still keep the dog's overall length. Just work on your blending.

Other times you'll have a customer get sniffy with you for refusing to brush out. You insist that the dog will have to be shaved. You explain it's unfair to put the dog through unnecessary suffering. That you abide by the Animal Welfare Act. So they say they'll go elsewhere. Maybe they will. If they find a willing groomer, then I am disappointed by that groomer.

Clipping off a badly matted dog still brings risks. You will need to take your time. And be extra careful with the clippers. Sometimes you can't see where the mat ends and the skin starts. There is a risk you may cut the dog in the process. So for this you'll need a tighter tooth blade like a 10 or 15. Or even a trimmer on a safe setting. This will help prevent the skin from accidentally feeding through the clipper blade.

You will also need to change blades frequently. The blades will get hot. You don't want to risk the hot blade touching the skin and causing clipper burn.

It will be impossible to determine the length of the end result on a badly matted dog. The blade has to go under the mat to remove it. So if the mats are too tight to the skin, it's going to be a short shave down.

You also can't anticipate the condition of the skin under the matting. The skin could already have pre-existing irritation, because of the mats.

Only by removing the mats will you be able to see the red angry blotches.

Of course, the customer might think these are your fault. So you'll have to explain before grooming that skin irritation is often a result of a neglected coat. You will be removing the mats and can't predict the condition of the skin underneath.

With serious matting I only groom the dog if the owner accepts that it will be a clip off.

As Precious likes to remind these customers: "It's hair. It grows back".

22. Snap-On Snap-Off

Has it happened to you? You're happily running the clipper along a dog's back. You're using a comb attachment (snap-on) on the blade. Suddenly the comb attachment flies off. And you've created a racing stripe. Instead of the even clip you were after.

It's happened to me. I cried blue murder. I swore I would never again use snap-ons.

But this was some years ago. Things have changed recently. In my humble opinion, it's thanks to Wahl for coming out with their metal models. These are a god-send. The problems I had with snap-ons are now a thing of the past. I'm converted. As are many of my colleagues. They, like me, thought of snap-ons as a troublesome waste of time.

So I now recommend using comb attachments. But remember. This is advice for dog groomers working in a commercial salon.

Snap-on combs help you achieve an even length. They help you work more time-efficiently. Sure, for purists this might not achieve the perfect scissored cut for shows and competitions. But working in a commercial salon isn't about show standards. As I say elsewhere, we are grooming people's pets. The priorities are 'different' than grooming for show and competition.

Yes you can use comb attachments on a 10, 15 or 30 blade. But I never use the metal attachment combs on a 40 blade. This is because of the risk of breaking the teeth on a 40.

My preference is a 30 blade under the attachment combs. But 10 or 15 is fine. Nothing is written in stone when using them. Use your own judgement. Perhaps start with a longer comb attachment. Then work your way down to the shorter ones. It may take a bit of trial and error. And some getting used to. But I recommend it for the time you'll save. And the ease that comb attachments can bring into your grooming.

23. Clipper Lines & Reverse Clipping

When grooming and using clippers, we all hate to see clipper lines. This is often the case with breeds like Westies or Spaniels. Normally when using 7F or 5F blades.

Sometimes the lines are really evident. The blade is cutting into the thick under-layer.

When clipping 'with the grain' you are 'chasing' the coat. This means the coat is being cut. But at the same time it's being pushed down.

So how to prevent clipper lines?

Here are some tips for helping to minimise these lines:

* you can use a carding tool. This will remove some of the undercoat and will make for an easier and smoother finish with the clipper blade.

* for heavier-coated breeds, you can use a coat king or similar product. A rake type tool will also help to remove undercoat.

* Use your blaster or high-velocity dryer to blast the undercoat out.

* Reverse clip.

To minimise lines, I like to Reverse clip.

Reverse clipping – which means clipping in the opposite direction of the coat - you are cutting under the coat. Closer to the hair shaft.

You've got to be careful. With reverse clipping you will always go shorter. So make sure you understand your blade lengths.

For example, a 7F with the grain would be a 4F or 5F Reverse, depending on the thickness of the coat.

However, if your dog does not have a thick coat to begin with, then there is no reason to reverse. Unless you're going for a very short look.

When reversing on a styled hair-cut you will have to blend in from long to short. For example, blending your legs into your body. So don't go too short. This will make the blending in more difficult. It will be harder to achieve a nice finish.

On a regular clip-down all over, or when the body is completely shaved, reverse clipping will make the haircut look more even. Just make sure you still follow the grain of the coat, but in reverse.

24. Clipper Irritation

I don't like to shave. Which is why I often have this really cool Miami Vice Don Johnson 5pm shadow. Okay, maybe it's more like five days of growth. And it starts to look scruffy.

So I give myself a clean shave. I end up with this horrible irritation on the skin. The more I scratch, the worse it gets.

Same applies with dogs. When a dog isn't used to getting clipped, it can get clipper irritation. Not to be confused with clipper burn.

Imagine having a lot of hair on one area for quite some time. Then suddenly it's removed. To a very short end result. A dog's first reaction normally is to lick it if they can. Or to scratch it. It's uncomfortable. It's sensitive. It stings a little bit.

The skin may also look reddish. A bit angry or sore. The owner may worry that their dog actually got clipper burn.

Clipper burn is when you've been using a blade for too long. The metal blade gets hot and can burn the dog's skin.

So this is something you need to be careful about. Make sure to change the blade regularly.

In most cases, the dog's skin reaction is clipper irritation.

At a men's barber shop you may notice the barber will often apply a soothing cream. Or a powder onto the neck line.

You can do the same. Apply a powder or anti-septic cream to areas of the dog's skin that look red or irritated. Tell the customer about it. Ask them to keep an eye out.

If the dog fusses over the area too much (licking, nibbling, scratching), it could lead to a hot spot. And then the risk of infection.

Update your records as well. Make a note that the dog's skin is prone to clipper irritation.

25. Clip-Off for Double Coated Breed

Chances are you've had a customer with a double-coated breed ask for a short cut. Or even a shave.

If you do this, you'll change the texture, possibly even the colour, of the coat. With some breeds it MAY - and, I repeat, MAY - ruin the coat. And stop it from growing normally. Samoyeds and Chows are especially prone to this.

That said, I wouldn't turn the customer away. First, I'll educate them about the possible consequences.

Then it's up to them. If they still insist, I'll do it. I might cry in my cornflakes for a week. Or live with the regret forevermore. But if I don't do it, somebody else will. I'd feel less guilty about it if the dog already had a thick, incorrect coat.

Generally, there are two reasons why the customer would like their double-coated breed shaved.

First, because they believe the dog's thick undercoat makes them hot.

In fact, the coat protects the dog from the elements. Including heat from the sun.

Ask the customer to imagine a house without insulation. In the warm summertime, the inside of the house would get warm. And in the cold winter time, the house would get cold. Think of the double-coat as a layer that, like insulation, helps regulate the dog's body temperature.

Second, because the dog is shedding too much hair. The way to remove dead hair (the hair that sheds) is simply a good bath and a dry with a blaster. Finish with a stand dryer and a thorough brushing out. This addresses the problem of shedding. Shaving the dog's coat in a double-coated breed won't resolve shedding. It might for a couple of weeks. After that, the dog will continue to shed.

Take a moment to consider the customer's lifestyle. Maybe they just don't have the time to maintain a double-coated breed. Going short could therefore be the solution for them. However disappointed we might be in ourselves. And maybe don't tell all your groomer friends on facebook what you've just done.

26. Combs & Combing

Okay, maybe not the most compelling subject. But I assure you. This is an area with a lot of teeth in it. Yes. That was a deliberate, horrible pun.

A comb is not just a comb. If you walk into a grooming supplier, you will see a significant variety of combs. There is a big difference in price and quality.

Generally, people will have a preference about the size of comb they are using. For example, a 'doll comb'. As the name suggests, it's a small comb.

I find small combs ideal for finding tangles or knots. Using them to loosen and remove the knots.

For the most part, I prefer a comb that has long enough teeth to penetrate the coat. To lift it correctly.

In my experience, long combs do this best. Your hand is further away from the coat. It is therefore not interfering with lifting the hair. It may take a little getting used to initially. But I recommend you try it. See the difference it makes.

Also, don't get lazy with your combing. You should be combing as often as every one or two minutes. Too many times I have watched a groomer style the whole dog and only use the comb a couple of times. I'm not surprised that once the dog shakes itself, there are a bunch of loose ends sticking out. Therefore, you need to be combing almost constantly during a groom. And keep a spray bottle of water nearby. This way you don't end up with static lift when you are combing so thoroughly.

When combing, put the comb into the hair with the teeth angled downwards. Turn the comb toward you and lift up. This will encourage the coat to stay up or out and not fall down right away.

To help keep the coat lifted up, you can use a scissoring spray. But don't be too trigger happy. Just a light mist from a distance. Don't make the coat wet.

Also, don't just comb the part you're scissoring. Use the comb everywhere across the body. Otherwise, you might have gone too short with your scissors. Use your comb as a tool to help keep your scissoring even.

27. Hand-Stripping

PRECIOUS: where there is controversy, I like to get involved. What can I say? A little bit of drama and excitement is intriguing.

So, if you haven't heard, there is a great big to-do right now about hand-stripping. The gloves are off (get it? 'hand stripping'? alright, groan, you've heard it before).

Okay, so maybe the controversy doesn't warrant a headline in the New York Times. But you will hear different opinions about hand-stripping. And these opinions can get a little heated.

At the salon, we get occasional phone calls from owners of Terriers – for example, Border, Fox, Airedale, Welsh. They ask if we know how to hand-strip.

They have taken advice from their breeder. They've been told that their new dog will require regular hand-stripping (or 'carding') once it's an adult. So they've contacted a few grooming salons. And discovered that not everybody hand-strips.

You may get requests from owners of Spaniels or Setters. Your gun dogs / sporting breeds. Generally, though, it will be owners of Terriers.

Hand-stripping is the removal of dead hair, or a certain layer, using a special hand-stripping tool and your thumb or fingers. The dead hair should pull out easily as you work your way over the dog's body.

This should be a relaxing process for the dog. It should feel good. The dog MAY even fall asleep while you are doing it.

If you're already a groomer, chances are you've come across hand-stripping. Perhaps at your school. A seminar. Or grooming competition.

Maybe you are an expert hand-stripper. And you're proud of this valuable skill. It adds a concrete benefit to your grooming business.

But hand-stripping is not an everyday method in a commercial grooming salon.

In my opinion, you should only offer hand-stripping under two conditions:

1. IF the dog has the right coat for it.
2. IF the dog is willing to accept it without any struggle.

By 'struggle' I mean that the dog doesn't like it. It's panting nervously. Squirming on the table. Trying to fend you off with its teeth.

Some Terrier breeders will say their dogs can take it "because they're Terriers". With all due respect to all good Terrier breeders, this is Hullabaloo.

Breeders are specialists. They know properly how to maintain a coat that requires regular hand-stripping. They keep on top of it on a daily or weekly basis.

But we can't expect the same discipline from the general pet owner.

I disagree with hand-stripping if it causes the dog pain and discomfort. It's not necessary. It goes against the Animal Welfare Act. Which says that we should not inflict pain on a dog unnecessarily. There is an option.

That's not to say I won't hand-strip a pet dog. But I'll talk to the customer first. They shouldn't be locked into the idea that hand-stripping is required just because of the dog's breed and coat.

If the dog is a household pet, it can be clipped instead. Visually you achieve the same result.

But doesn't clipping change the coat texture? And colour? Maybe the customer really likes their dog with its bristly, wiry coat?

Well, yes. The coat will lose its texture. Soften. And the colour will change.

This happens when you clip with a short blade. It cuts into the hair shaft. If you add a comb attachment, it will minimise the loss of texture or softening of the coat. The colour will be less affected.

I'm happy to make concessions. Because you've got to be flexible about these things.

I'll hand-strip a Border happily, provided it's not painful for the dog. And the dog is well-behaved on the table. I also make sure it comes at least twice a year for a full hand-strip. With maybe the occasional light tidy-up hand-strip in between.

And here's a second concession. But it comes with a compromise. I also see a lot of Fox Terriers. I will hand-strip the colour. But I'll clip the white with an attachment comb (eg. dark blue over a 30). The white hair is more stable and will normally grow back the same. However, it may be a lot thicker and curlier. You may want to card or coat king the white first because this will help maintain some texture.

One more thing. Spaying or neutering changes a dog's coat. So it's not necessary for the owner of a fixed dog to request hand-stripping just because they think this is required for the coat.

If you operate a commercial dog grooming salon that, in the main, serves general pets (i.e. not show dogs) then there is no real reason to offer hand-stripping.

The customer has to appreciate that hand-stripping is a specialist skill. Some breeds, like the Border Terrier, are easy. But a Wire-Hair Fox Terrier or a Scottie could take years to master. Not every groomer can offer, therefore, hand-stripping to a high standard. Moreover, it can take a lot of extra time. Your pricing will need to reflect this.

Sure, from a purely business perspective, you might like to offer hand-stripping. But it's not necessary. You don't have to think of yourself as any less a groomer for not offering it.

28. General Dog Handling

It's often said that HALF of dog grooming is being a good dog handler. Yes, it's a huge part of our success. You can't clip or scissor very well if you can't control the dog.

So you have to achieve a co-operative rapport with your dog. A kind of mutual respect. The dog must know that it is not here for playtime. Rather, the dog is here for the serious business of getting a haircut. Hopefully, a good one.

Which is not to say that I'm not friendly or interactive with the dog before or after grooming. Of course I am. And some dogs I just really love to bits.

But when the dog is in the bath or on the table, I focus. I am calm. I am assertive.

A student said to me once: "Colin, you look like a grumpy drill sergeant."

I was in the middle of scissoring legs on a Miniature Schnauzer.

I had to stop. And giggle. I would have made a good soldier I think. Sergeant Taylor has a nice ring to it.

"That's because I'm concentrating," I explained.

It's true though. When I have a dog in the bath or on the table, this is not playtime. So I put on my serious face. I handle the dog with deliberate movements. My actions are purposeful. It looks like I am emotionally disconnected.

Often I'll have new students heap loads of Big Affection on a dog during grooming. They'll nuzzle it under the chin. Kiss it on the nose. Scratch its tummy. Make the strangest noises.

My students will know my position on Big Affection. On cutesy-wutesy doggie-speak.

First of all, it's not your job to heap Big Affection on a dog while you're grooming. The dog has a family. Let them be the ones to shower the dog with affection.

Second, high-pitched squeals and mushy appeals can unsettle the dog. Or make the dog interactive. Cause him to move around on the table. Or confuse him because suddenly he thinks it's playtime.

But you don't want to 'play' with the dog during grooming. This wastes time. If you count up every minute of Big Affection, at the end of the day that's a lot of lost minutes.

At the end of the week that's five or six times more lost minutes.

Plus it increases the risk of an accident happening.

29. Calm. Assertive.

When I dreamt of becoming a dog groomer, I would imagine myself in a smart establishment. Parading a perfectly mannered Poodle into the salon. He would obediently allow me to lift him into the bath. Later, he would stand perfectly still like a gentleman on the table. I would create beautiful shapes with my scissors.

This mental image didn't survive my first day in a professional salon. I was startled by a Golden Doodle thrashing about wildly. Slamming on the brakes as soon as I took him by the lead. Making horrific crying noises. Like he was about to get murdered.

I tried to appeal to him. I told him "it's okay Freddy, I'm not going to kill you". I massaged his ears gently. I whispered sweet nothings. I put him at ease. And I thought, that's it, I'm a dog whisperer. This is my natural calling. I have a gift.

Two seconds later, as soon as I coaxed him along, he started throwing his body about and squealing.

My boss came over. She took the dog firmly by his collar. And marched him directly into the salon.

She was like an old-fashioned school mistress. Taking an unruly child by the ear into the Principal's office.

My instructor refused to indulge the dog's whimpering and anxiety. Instead, she was calm, assertive and firm. The dog just simply fell into line. And she did it all so efficiently. With purpose. I was impressed.

Having control of a dog requires this calm, assertive authority. We need this most when clipping or scissoring the dog on the table.

When a dog starts to get fidgety, I tell her to 'stop'. I move her gently, but with purpose, back into position. Usually by guiding her head from under her chin.

You should generally be able to control the dog with your hands to the chest. Or between the rear legs. If she is difficult to control, you might have to be a little more hands-on.

But you have to be careful. You don't want to injure the dog. The dog may have spinal or back problems. Perhaps joint issues. Make sure you don't push the dog back into position with sudden or jerky movements. Any handling of the limbs – for example, taking hold of a paw to clip the nails - must always be a natural movement. Don't pull the leg away in an awkward direction.

Yes, it gets tricky if the dog doesn't co-operate. If you're getting frustrated, you might start to mutter really bad words. You might explode and yell at the dog. You might push the dog angrily because you've lost your patience.

If you feel yourself going there, stop. Take a breath. Count to ten.

Dogs are intuitive, soulful creatures. They can feel your anger and frustration. This will unsettle them. They need to be re-assured that you are in control. That their environment is safe.

Try placing your hand on the dog's shoulder blades. This helps to calm the dog. And it asserts your authority.

Now, try again. If the dog is still wriggling about, insert two fingers firmly in the neck strap. This may stop the dog moving about too much.

If you're still not getting anywhere, ask for some help from a colleague. If you're on your own, slow down. Although it might take ages before you can finish the groom.

Depending on your situation, you may ask the owner to help hold the dog during grooming. Or you can decide that, regretfully, you are unable to groom the dog.

Don't beat yourself up about it. In general, you'll be able to groom most dogs. And with experience, your handling will improve. You'll learn to anticipate the dog's movements. You will handle your dog with purpose.

30. Dog Fight

There is no reason why dogs should have to mix with each other in your grooming salon. So you shouldn't ever have dogs fight.

You might run day-care with your salon. But keep this separate. And make sure the dogs are well-socialised. That they get on with each other.

As for your salon area, install some eye-hooks into the sides of the walls. Dogs that are waiting can simply be secured to the eye hooks. Just make sure there is enough room between these hitching stations so that the dogs can't reach each other.

You might also have cages / crates in your salon. Or specially built holding cells. That's fine. Dogs can wait there.

Manage your bookings tightly. Minimise the amount of time a dog is in your care.

Despite these things, dogs may sometimes meet. And not like each other. And a fight breaks out.

We keep Pet Corrector in the salon. It's a can of compressed air. It emits a sharp hiss-like sound. Like a snake. If two dogs start brawling, I'll immediately try to pull one of them away by its collar. But if I can't get in there without risking injury, I'll spray the Pet Corrector.

A tin with marbles in it is also an option. I'll throw it onto the floor with force to startle the dogs.

In that split second, I'll grab one of the dogs by the collar and pull it away. Hopefully I'll have an assistant or colleague grab the other dog.

It's important therefore to make sure dogs are ALWAYS wearing their collars before and after grooming. So you've got something to grab them by.

Once the dogs have calmed down, I'll have to inspect them closely for any injuries. When a dog bites, the teeth can create a deep cut. The dog will need to see the vet if it has a bite. The vet will clean the injury. Likely stitch it up. And prescribe antibiotics to prevent infection.

When a dog comes to your salon, it's your responsibility to make sure it stays safe from harm.

You're not doing this simply for the sake of the dog. You don't want to risk a dog getting injured. Because then you'll have a dog in pain. You'll have to go to the vet. You may have to pay an expensive bill. And you'll have an upset customer.

It's worth never getting complacent about dogs coming in and out of the grooming salon. Because it can really ruin your day if there's a fight.

31. Dogs That Bite

COLIN: I have a few battle scars. I'd like to say they come from my time as a green beret. Sergeant Taylor. Deployed on secret missions to save the world from terrorists. But they don't. I just got unlucky a few times with some dogs. Dogs that bite.

PRECIOUS: I love that image of Colin as a green beret. But really, it's me who should be in uniform. I own this subject. So, battle-hardened by warfare in the trenches, let me tell you about dogs that bite.

There are two types. You have the so-called fear biters, which can include submissive biters. And you have the aggressive biters. It's worth understanding the difference. And being able to read the signs.

The fear biters aren't vicious. They're afraid. They have two responses. Fight or Flight. If they cannot flee or run away, they will fight. They are defending themselves with their God-given means: their teeth.

When a customer arrives, the dog may already be demonstrating whether or not it will co-operate in the bath or the grooming table. Obvious signals include tail between the legs. An unwillingness to come into the shop. Braking with all of its legs. A stooped, suspicious look at you and the surroundings.

When you reach for the dog it may snap at you. To warn you off.

At other times, the dog won't give any warning signs. You lift it into the bath. Or onto the table. Suddenly it turns on you. The dog is scared. It is reacting to the situation.

The risk is that your hand, fingers or face get in the way.

Then there are the aggressive biters. These are the problem dogs. They have problems with their owners. Other groomers. With the vet.

You must always get a dog's history before booking. Confirm that the dog is used to grooming. That it is socialised well with people and other dogs.

Colin likes a bit of a challenge. He often tries to groom all dogs. Even the ones other groomers have refused. But then, he gained a bit of a reputation for being able to handle aggressive dogs.

He's a softie that way. And maybe it wasn't too clever after all. Because, frankly, they require extra time. Attention. Organising. Plus, he has the scars to prove it hasn't always worked out as well as he hoped.

So, I'm not sure I can recommend Colin's approach for everyone. Instead, I suggest the following:

* only groom dogs you can handle without having to call Emergency Services.

* use a muzzle. If that doesn't work, tell the customer you tried your best. You cannot take the risk of a bite.

* assert your authority over the dog. Don't make eye contact. Handle the dog with calm assertiveness. Let them know who is in charge.

* make a business decision. You would like to help the pleading owner and groom the dog for its own benefit. But if you get a bite, you could be out of work for the next week or more. One dog is not worth that risk. You can say No.

* always get the dog's history. You have to know what to expect. The customer might not be completely forthcoming. If you're not comfortable, don't do it.

* keep the grooming simple. Especially for the first groom. An easy-to-maintain cut like a 5F all over with a cute face (if you can).

* if the owner would like their dog shaped and scissored, suggest leaving this for now. You can do it in the future. After you've gained the dog's trust. But not for the first groom.

* praise the dog when it's doing well. But be calm and assertive when it needs to behave. Don't overdo the praise. Generally keep a quiet control over the dog.

* arrange an appointment when the salon is less busy. Keep all distractions to a minimum.

* never, ever, strike a dog in anger. You might be getting frustrated because the dog is testing you. If you feel your stress levels are about to go through the roof, chill-ax. Step outside for some fresh air. Grab a cup of coffee. Talk to a colleague about the X-Factor results. Indulge your suspicion it's all fixed. That usually calms me down.

32. Dog Bite

PRECIOUS: Let's look at what happens if a dog bites you. Colin doesn't do well with pain and blood. It's time for a true professional.

Despite our best efforts, we might get unlucky. We might end up with a dog bite. It could be serious. Or not. Slightly depends on the size of the dog. The severity of the bite.

Either way, you will likely be startled when it happens. And it might hurt like heck. If you can, get immediate assistance from a colleague. Have them take over your dog. With extreme caution!

Meanwhile, you need to get to the first aid kit. Run your cut under cold running water. Apply first aid as necessary. Feel free to swear at this moment. It helps relieve some of the pain.

Now, what about the dog and the customer? You might be angry and frustrated, but the dog's welfare is still your responsibility. So make sure the dog is secured. Off the table. Or out of the bath. I have a section later on about 'Unattended Dogs' and what to do.

Your bite might be just a scratch. If you think you can still manage without further risk of injury, then finish the grooming. But if it's a serious bite you have to stop.

Contact the customer. Explain what happened.

If you didn't get anywhere with the grooming, don't charge anything. With regret, the dog will have to be seen by somebody else. Or groomed by the vet.

If you got part way through the grooming, you'll have to make a business decision. I might ask for half the amount. If the customer objects, explain that a dog bite is not your fault. You booked the dog in good faith. On the assumption there wouldn't be a problem. If the customer doesn't pay, you are out of pocket, plus you've got an injury. You might even miss a few days grooming and income.

If the customer still refuses, this is one for your Blacklist. We take a look at blacklisting in the next section of the book.

If the customer gets rude and upset, I would cut my losses. I don't need the aggravation of a scene in my salon. So I'll give in and open the door for them to leave. Then I'll add their details to my Blacklist.

As for the dog, it might not allow you or your colleague to get close to it without risking another bite. You might need your customer to come into the salon to collect the dog.

Your customer might be upset and apologetic. I am sympathetic. They are trying to do the right thing for their dog. They love their dog. They can't bear to know that Mr. Muffin has a vicious side.

As to whether or not you're willing to see this customer again, refer to the section about 'dogs that bite'. In most cases, the dog is biting the situation. Biting at the brush. Or the clippers. And your hand just got in the way. They aren't aggressively attacking.

You cannot equate this to the uncontrolled dog that bites a postal worker or a child playing in a park. Use common sense. Don't be alarmist. Don't be a Diva. You will live to groom another day.

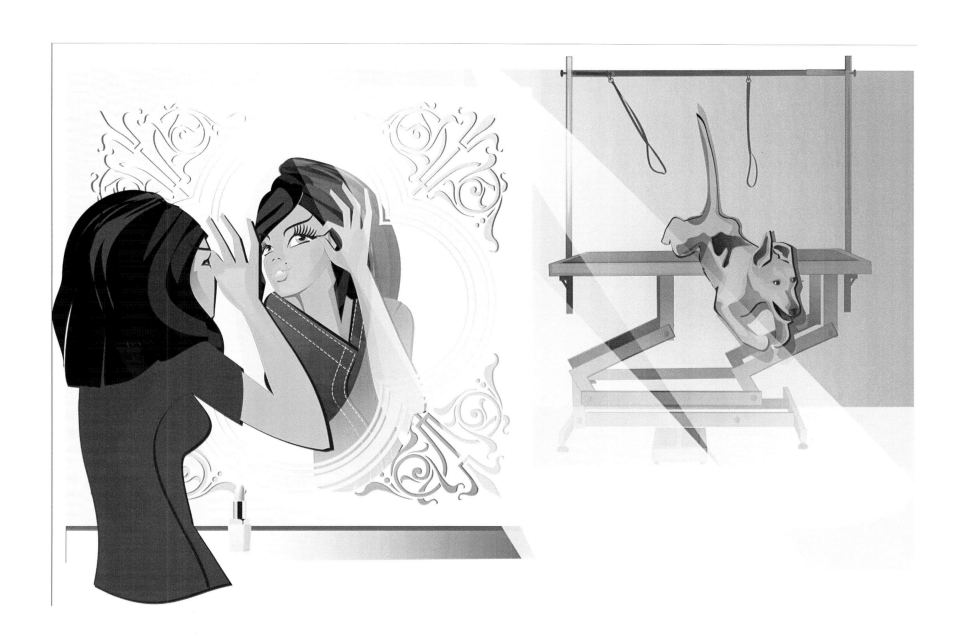

33. Dog Left Unattended

The second of my six rules for the grooming salon is never to leave a dog unattended.

This applies anywhere in the salon. A dog that is secured to the table might get distracted. Jump off. And hang itself from the table restraint.

A dog in the bath could try to scrabble out. The bath is slippery. The dog may slip. Bang its head. Its legs may go in opposite directions. And it will end up with a dislocated joint.

If the dog is running around loose, it may mark its territory everywhere. Which is clearly less serious. But aggravating.

But things happen. The telephone rings. A customer distracts you. A delivery arrives.

We turn our backs for a minute. And disaster.

With my students, I carry out a short, but effective drill. I put on my little green beret. The student is at the table with their dog. And I bark out the command 'Secure!'

Immediately, the student has to unleash their dog from the table. And move it to a secure hitching station in the salon. Or into a crate.

I make them do this several times. It's not a power-trip moment for me. Indulging my little Army fantasies. It's an important lesson. They need automatically to get into the habit of securing a dog. Making sure it is never left unattended in a vulnerable position. Too much is at risk.

34. Dog Has a Seizure During Grooming

PRECIOUS: Seizures in dogs during grooming are not uncommon. So, you'll need to know what to do. You'll have to be an action heroine when it happens. Which is why I've told Colin to put the kettle on. To take a break.

The responsible dog owner will inform you that their dog is epileptic. Or prone to seizures or panic attacks. Make sure you've marked the dog's card with this. Highlight it in your appointments book. We can really do without these surprises.

A seizure occurs because of abnormal flashes of electric waves in the brain. The dog could be epileptic. The dog might have a brain tumour. Or the seizure could be a one-off, completely random incident.

During a seizure, the dog's eyes may appear to roll back. Its legs may go rigid. Its body may start to convulse uncontrollably. The dog may gnash its teeth. It could lose control of its bowels.

There aren't really any warning signs before a seizure happens. One second the dog could be playing with you. Or standing like a gentleman on the table. The next second it could be seizing.

So, here's what action heroine Precious does:

I lay the dog on the floor immediately. Clear the space around it. Remove any objects that might get in the way. Or could cause injury.

I make sure to keep other dogs separate. They will be very curious to know what's going on. They may react badly.

I try to keep the dog on its side with its airways clear. You can hold onto the dog firmly, but gently, at the side of the neck. But away from its teeth. This is to keep the dog's head secure so it doesn't accidentally thrash against the floor. Or elsewhere.

Don't worry about the dog 'swallowing its tongue'. This won't happen. There is no need to hold its tongue. Or put any objects in its mouth.

If possible, I'll put down some blankets. To make the area around the dog a bit softer until it emerges from its seizure.

The seizure may last for a few minutes. It's best to contact the owner immediately if practical. If the owner is accustomed to the dog's seizures, they may offer additional advice. If the owner was unaware, they might freak out a little bit. Reassure the owner that the dog is fine. But arrangements should be made to take their dog to the vet.

If the seizure lasts more than ten minutes, the dog should definitely see the vet.

While the dog is still seizing, soften the lights. Turn off all other noise like loud blasters or your Metallica CD. I'll say some nice re-assuring things to the dog. Perhaps squeeze its paws. Give it some tactile comfort. I will speak to the dog in a gentle voice.

The dog will emerge not knowing what has happened. It might feel nauseous. Groggy. Wobbly. It may vomit. Or be unable to walk steadily for a few minutes.

Praise the dog, but quietly. Once the dog is settled, make sure the owner has been informed. Try to record the duration of the seizure. The owner needs to share this information with the vet.

The owner will understandably be worried by your report. You can tell them it's not uncommon for dogs to have seizures (about three in every 100 dogs). Many epileptic dogs will have full and long happy lives. My friend Christian's epileptic Cocker Spaniel lived for a happy, healthy 15 years.

And that's about all you need to say. I would resist speculating on possible causes. That's the vet's job. The vet is likely to order a bunch of tests. Plus a diagnostic assessment with a specialist. Potentially a brain scan.

So the question you might still have is this: if I only got part way through the grooming and the dog is now settled down, do I continue grooming? If not, what do I charge the customer?

Here's my answer: if you only got part way through the grooming, charge half-price. Agree with the customer to finish the dog another day. You've probably all been through quite enough today.

If you hadn't started the grooming, then don't charge anything. But when you re-book, ask that the customer pay the full price up-front. Just in case there is a repeat of the incident. They should understand.

Of course, you'll need to be diplomatic and sensitive about this. You don't want to come across looking frustrated about the money. It's really all about the dog's welfare right now. You want to make sure that's how your customer sees it too.

If you only got part way through the cut, the dog might get laughed at by all his pals in the park. In a lot of cases, the dog will have settled down and look fit again. So, with the owner's consent, just do a quick tidy-up. Book another appointment when you can finish properly.

35. Cutting or Injuring a Dog

It happens to the best of us. We take the scissor blade too close to an ear we are tidying up and, slice. The scissor has struck the dog's ear. It's bleeding.

The first thing to do is apply a clean wet towel. Apply pressure to the cut area. Keep doing this until the bleeding stops. If the bleeding stops quickly, inspect the severity of the cut. It might just be a tiny superficial nick. And the dog's skin may already be starting to close after just a few minutes. You can apply some alcohol-free iodine to the cut. When the owner comes to collect their dog, explain what happened. The treatment you provided. Ask them to keep an eye on the cut over the next few days.

Depending on the severity, the customer may still choose to get the vet to take a look. If it's a tiny superficial cut it may not be necessary. A mother wouldn't necessarily take her daughter to the doctor for a scraped knee from falling off her bicycle. With dogs - who are prone to getting minor bumps and cuts because of actively playing in parks and bushes outdoors - it's only the hypochondriac owner who needs to see the vet for something so minor.

However, if the cut is a little more serious and continues to bleed, the dog will need to be taken to the vet. You must continue applying pressure with a clean wet towel. Change the towel frequently. You can also use paper towel for this. The aim is to stop the bleeding. And to prevent infection. So make sure the wet towel you are using is clean.

Get somebody to help you through this. Perhaps another groomer. Tell them to put down whatever they are doing. Secure all other dogs in the salon. Stick a note to the front of your shop that you'll be back in 30 minutes. Apologise for the inconvenience.

Right now, this dog and this situation require your full attention. Without the distraction of other customers or dogs.

Stay calm. Breathe.

The dog's welfare is paramount here. You don't want to transfer your anxiety onto the dog. Go through the motions calmly and professionally.

Now, contact the owner. Explain what happened. Find out who their vet is. Ideally you'll already have this information on your customer record. If practical, you'll want to take the dog to its own vet. They will have its records on file. Contact the vet. Let them know you are on your way. Make sure the dog can be seen immediately. The vet will have a protocol in place for emergencies.

Now, take the dog to the vet. The owner may be able to take the dog. Personally, though, I prefer to be there. To be fully aware of everything that is happening. Even if it screws up the rest of my day.

Take it from there. Vets are good at being able to treat emergencies like this. They've seen it all before. And they will put the customer at ease.

What to do about your customer?

In those instances where you, the groomer, have accidentally cut the dog – for example, your scissors sliced the dog's ear or its tail or one of the dog's pads - and the accident could have been avoided, you need to take responsibility.

If the cut is so minor it doesn't require a vet's attention, I suggest you still ask for the full grooming fee. But offer a discount off their next appointment. Remember, this applies only if the cut is tiny, superficial and harmless.

If the cut is serious, and the accident is clearly your fault (i.e. not the customer's fault, not the dog's fault), again you need to take full responsibility.

Nine times out of ten, HOWEVER, a cut happens because of having to clip a matted dog. And this is a whole other ball game. And something I get my knickers in a twist about. Imagine me now with my grumpy face.

When we clip a badly matted dog, we are actually providing a treatment for a neglected dog. But it's difficult. It's hard to see where the mat stops and the skin starts. So there is increased risk of an accidental cut.

Before you start therefore, you need to have a delicate conversation with the customer. Indicate that you will have to charge extra because you need to be extra careful. It will take more time. Because they've allowed their dog to get into this state, there is a risk of the clipper nicking the dog's skin.

They have the option of course of going to the vet to do the grooming instead. Which will cost a lot more. And may involve having to sedate the dog. They can go to another groomer. Or they can get their dog groomed by you.

At this stage, you can ask the owner to sign a waiver. They need to agree not to hold you responsible for an accidental cut because of their own neglect of the dog's coat.

Sounds a little heavy-handed. Maybe it's not the most customer-friendly. But I have heard too often of instances when an owner takes a badly matted dog into the salon. The groomer tries their best to please the customer. Then accidentally cuts the dog's skin with the clippers.

The owner then gets all indignant and upset that the groomer cut their dog. Somehow, this is the groomer's fault.

It's not. And you should not apologise for accidentally nicking the skin of a badly matted dog. We wouldn't be in this situation in the first place if the owner had not neglected their dog.

You'll have to explain all this diplomatically of course.

36. Ear (Aural) Hematoma

I watch a little bit of TV every now and then. Okay. Maybe more than average. Over the years I've seen a lot of commercials. I always notice the ones with dogs shaking their heads after a bath. Or after they've run through sprinklers in the summer sun.

The camera will do that slow-motion thing. There will be a million droplets flying everywhere. And then you're told to go out and buy a certain type of dog food. Because if you want your dog to look and feel this good, then only Brand-X will do.

Those commercials always throw me for a loop. Instead of droplets of water flying everywhere, I see blood.

This isn't me getting all dark and moody. I have a point. It has to do with ear (aural) hematoma.

Barney was an Old English Sheepdog. He came to the salon with badly matted ears. After I shaved the ears, he shook his head. Again and again. He was probably feeling the incredible relief of having his ears clipped short.

Then suddenly, a spray of blood. Across the salon wall. Across my chest. And face. Like something out of a Tarantino movie.

I was shocked. Immediately, I thought I had cut him. But I wasn't handling scissors. And I had finished with the clippers. I wondered what the heck just happened.

Barney had somehow banged the tip of his ear flap so hard, it burst a blood vessel. I didn't know this at the time. I was too confused and alarmed.

I applied a clean wet towel, with pressure, to Barney's ear.

My assistant contacted the owner. She informed them that Barney's ear was bleeding.

Naturally, their assumption was that I cut Barney. After all, he's in the salon. We have lots of sharp objects.

My assistant agreed with the owners that we meet at the vet.

PRECIOUS: Stop the presses. Who is Colin kidding? I'm the one who jumps into action. And there is a very good reason for this. Which I'll show you in a second. Us ladies might just have an advantage over the men handling this one.

Provided Colin hasn't fainted from the blood, first thing I do is inspect the ear flap carefully. I make doubly sure it's not a cut from my clippers. That I haven't accidentally cut the dog.

I hold a clean wet towel, with pressure to the ear to stop the bleeding. Once it stops, I lift the dog's ears (both ears) above its head. I apply some gauze to keep the ears in place on top of the head.

Then I whip off my tights (nylons). I grab a pair of scissors. Plenty of those around. I cut the toe out of the foot to create a kind of nylon tube. I take this and slip it over the dog's face and head. This will hold the ears in position, folded over the top of its head.

Then we go to the vet.

In Barney's case, everything was explained. The matting. The ears being shaved. The vigorous head shaking.

The vet's diagnosis? Ear (aural) hematoma. Caused by the dog shaking its head.

She explained that it can often happen to dogs with ear infection. They shake their head to seek relief from the pain of infection. They bang the tips of their ears against something and it causes bruising. A pool of blood will form. But instead of bursting and spraying blood, the blood can clot. It then creates this firm swelling. If it isn't treated, the dog ends up with a thick, bumpy ear. Which is often described as 'cauliflower ear'.

I'd seen dogs before with cauliflower ear. But never understood what causes it. Now I knew.

The owners were likewise intrigued. They were happy to see that Barney would be okay. And they promised to come in more often. To make sure his ears didn't get so badly matted in future.

37. Pregnant Bitch

PRECIOUS: It's hardly surprising that Colin would ask me to write this piece. He claims to have selected my topics randomly. But I don't believe him for a second.

During a pre-grooming consultation, always ask the owner if there is anything you need to know. If the dog was recently in season, they should let you know. But ask anyway. Ask if she was mated.

If the answer is yes, then you might have a pregnant bitch.

The most stressful part of grooming a pregnant dog is the bathing and drying. It's also the most time-consuming. I try to minimise the amount of time that a pregnant bitch is in the salon. So I will ask the owner to take care of the bathing and drying at home.

I have heard of dogs miscarrying in the bath. Or miscarrying afterwards because of the stress of a bath. This is a risk you don't want to take.

A professional breeder will already know this. They wouldn't take their pregnant bitch to the groomer for a bath and blow-dry. The general pet owner, however, will benefit from your advice.

I am reluctant to groom a pregnant bitch because of the potential for complications. I am more comfortable if it's only been a couple of weeks since the mating. Assuming that the customer has volunteered the information. Some people won't even know that their dog is pregnant.

But if they do know, or suspect, I won't take her if it's been four weeks or more since the first mating. For that in-between period of three / four weeks, I will take the dog into the salon, but only for a simple dry cut. No bath. No blow dry.

I also have to feel that the dog is calm and good on the table. I will only aim to achieve a short and easy-to-manage cut.

I would use my trimmer around the teats because this is better for hygiene once the puppies arrive. But I'll try to get through this quickly. Let's call it a 'maintenance' cut. I want to minimise the time the dog is on the table. And keep her stress level to a minimum.

If the dog arrived at the salon already stressed out, I would unfortunately, have to say no. Even if it's just to clean up the area around her nipples. I'll suggest they take her to the vet instead.

38. Obese Dog

PRECIOUS: You are bound to come across a dog that is obese. Or seriously overweight. Their owners allow it to eat too much. The dog isn't getting any exercise.

Apart from a legitimate medical reason, there is no excuse for an obese dog. It's not like it can raid the fridge in the middle of the night. Take the car to a McDonald's drive-thru. Or call the pizza guy for a deep-pan double Pepperoni. Extra cheese.

An obese dog can have all kinds of health complications. Its breathing might be laboured. It could be on a terrible diet that is causing skin irritation. It can develop problems with its joints.

The owner is, simply, neglecting their dog. They're usually not paying too much attention to other areas of the dog's health either.

The dog's nails could be overgrown. Its ears infected. It might have fleas because the treatments haven't been kept up. Its coat might be full of mats because it isn't being brushed.

The good news is this: they have come to the salon. By this, the owner is, at last, doing the right thing.

It's up to you how you'd like to handle the customer. Do you get all ballistic and indignant and preachy at them? Call the RSPCA? It is animal cruelty after all.

I try to find out what's going on first.

I'll ask why the dog is obese. Maybe it has problems with its thyroid gland. Maybe the owner is really distressed about its obesity. She has been to the vet a hundred times. And is honestly, actively trying to do something. Maybe the dog has recently been rescued.

But if the owner is blissfully unaware that there is a problem, I will say something.

I'll tell the owner that their dog needs to go on a diet. I'll ask them if they are aware of the health complications. I'll recommend they see their vet. Because if they don't do something about it, their dog could get seriously ill.

Some customers have reacted badly. I've been told to back off and mind my own business. Not in those words.

If you want to keep the peace, perhaps make polite suggestions about better food alternatives.

A friend of mine uses a different tactic. She doesn't say anything until the pre-grooming consultation. She'll go through the normal motions. Inspect the coat. Check the feet. That sort of thing.

And then she will ask 'how many months?'

The customer is thrown. They don't understand.

So my friend elaborates. "How many months has the vet given your dog? You know... to live?"

It's a 'cruel to be kind' moment.

The customer may not know how to answer. They might be seriously offended. But at least they've been confronted with the prospect of their dog's early death. Because of obesity.

They love their dog. My friend knows this. But they're feeding it too many treats. There are other ways of showing affection. So my friend wants to shake them out of their complacency.

You have to be fair about this. I'm not talking about an overweight dog that is otherwise healthy. I am talking about really big, clinically obese dogs. We rarely see them. But sometimes we do. Use the means necessary to make the owner take positive action for the sake of their dog.

39. Old Dogs

A Yorkshire Terrier comes to me on a regular basis. Dandy is almost 20 years old.

To start, I place Dandy on the table and take a 5F on him. I wash him gently. Then wrap him in a towel. I take the stand dryer. I direct the warm air onto him. I rub his coat with the towel, and use a soft brush. Afterwards, I clip him again. Then I scissor his head and tail. He looks good. Not amazing. But good is good enough.

You get the picture. I am taking extra special care grooming an old dog.

We often see dogs of an incredible age. We remark how sprightly they still look and behave. But many old dogs will suffer from ailments. They may have poor eyesight. They can't really see what's going on. As a defence mechanism, they may snap at the person handling them. They may have tired joints that cause them pain. Their skin may have lots of moles that are prone to getting cut accidentally. They may have breathing difficulties.

It all becomes a bit of a worry. We have real, warranted concerns that the old dog may suffer a stroke. Or heart attack. We will be reluctant to groom. The last thing we want is for the dog to die in our care. Understandably, it's a risk we would rather avoid.

I do three things.

One: I ask the owner to stay at the salon for the duration of the session. The owner will see that I am handling their dog gently. That I haven't done anything upsetting. For example, don't take a high powered blaster to the dog. If the dog does start getting stressed (panting hard, losing control of its bowels), the owner can offer comfort immediately.

Two: if the dog is frail, I ask the owner to sign a simple waiver. You can find an example of one on my Academy website. In it, the owner acknowledges the dog's old age and poor health. It absolves the groomer of responsibility if the worst were to happen.

Three: I minimise the number of potential hazards for the old dog. I will ask the owner to bathe their dog themselves at home first. I book the dog at a time when the salon is less busy. I plan the grooming to take the least amount of time possible.

I am not aiming to achieve a perfect show cut. I am aiming for a good tidy-up that helps the dog look good. Feel good. All of this I explain to the owner. Because I have a process, the owner is reassured I know what I'm doing. It gives them confidence in my professionalism.

40. A Dog Has Died in My Care

I just finished brushing the Chow. I was pleased with the result. He looked incredible. About four years old. A rust orange lustrous coat. A happy, child-like temperament.

He was standing on the table when he collapsed.

His barrel chest landed with a soft, single thud. His legs splayed in awkward directions beneath his weight. His head rolled to one side. And hung slightly over the edge of the table.

I stepped backwards in shock. But reacted instinctively. I immediately lifted him off the table. I laid him on the floor. Cleared some space.

My assistant clocked what was happening. She quickly secured the dog she was bathing.

She contacted the vet. We were on our way.

She contacted the owners. Explained what just happened. Instructed them to meet us at the vet.

I carried the Chow in my arms and raced to my car. Minutes later we were at the vet.

She was already outside waiting. She took us straight through to the examination room.

The owner arrived. She had an accusing, bewildered look in her eyes.

We watched helplessly while the vet attempted Cardio-Pulmonary Resuscitation (CPR).

But nothing. The dog could not be revived.

The vet looked to the owner. And shook her head sadly.

The owner rushed over. She buried her face and tears in the dog's thick red mane.

I edged out of the examination room. I was shocked. Dumb-founded.

Just moments before, I had been in the salon. Everything was lively and loud. Dogs playing. The phone ringing. Customers chatting.

And suddenly, I was sitting by myself in the waiting area at the vet. This young, strong Chow was now lifeless on the vet's table.

I recall an eerie stillness. Any noise was muffled into a deep, quiet hum. It was as though the world around me stopped. In reverence for the departing spirit of this beautiful dog.

Moments later, the owner's husband arrived. The vet met him immediately. And took him to join his wife, and their dog.

I spoke to the vet. A Post Mortem would need to take place.

I went back to the salon. My assistant had cancelled all remaining appointments for the day. We closed. And hung up a sign. Apologising for the inconvenience.

In the days that followed, I spoke to the owners. They had a lot of questions for me. But I had no answers.

The dog was young. Fit. Healthy. Playful. No signs of distress or discomfort. He was a regular. So he was accustomed to grooming. I had not seen anything different from the times he had come in previously.

They, likewise, had not seen any indication of a problem.

We would have to wait for the results of the Post Mortem.

The vet contacted me a week later. She had already spoken to the owners. The Chow had died of a Massive Heart Attack. It was brought on by an undetected heart defect, likely from birth. There were no external contributing factors.

For a week I had lived with the anxiety that I had done something wrong. That my grooming caused the dog's sudden death. Was the salon temperature too high? Did I take too long brushing him out? Did I stress the dog somehow?

I was relieved therefore by the vet's report. And her consoling words. She was kind and sympathetic.

The owners contacted me shortly afterward. They were still grieving. But they wanted to reassure me that it was not my fault. They were grateful I tried to help their dog. They took consolation from knowing that he loved coming to us for his regular bath and brush. That he died without suffering. Among friends who truly loved him.

This is a hard story to tell. And I debated whether or not to include it in this book. I worried it might frighten an aspiring groomer from learning our trade.

In thirty years, this has been the only dog that has died on my table. Chances are very slim of this happening. But it can happen.

My advice therefore is to be vigilant. Minimise the risk of a dog dying in your care. I discuss this in other places. Like the section on grooming an old dog.

You have to know how to react in an emergency.

Be thorough in your pre-grooming consultation.

Watch for any signals from the dog that it might be unwell.

Don't use a blaster if it is too stressful.

In this case, the dog's collapse was out of my control. I responded by getting the dog to the vet immediately. I did everything I could. But I did not allow the dog's death to defeat me.

About a year later, the owners came back to the salon. They had an introduction to make. A sixteen-week old Chow. A female. Her name was Brandy. They wanted to book Brandy's first Puppy Bath.

41. Non-Groomers Opening a Salon

Here in London in the UK, I have seen one grooming salon open after another. It's really taken off in the last few years. In many cases, though, these salons have been open by people who aren't groomers themselves. Or they know little about the industry.

They might have worked in the City. For the media. Or in the military. They might have dropped out of school at 16. Or graduated from Cambridge. You just can't guess at their background.

But the thing is, they're not dog groomers. They are in business. They might be passionate dog lovers. And they chose to combine that passion with business. To open a dog grooming shop. Everybody likes working with dogs, right? Plus, there must be good money in it. We keep hearing in the media that the dog industry is recession-proof.

When people spend less money on shoes or cocktails or travel, they'll still spend money on their dogs. Maybe even more so.

These new business owners might not know anything about dog grooming initially. In time, however, they will learn. Often they have impeccable taste when it comes to designing their pet boutique. And they're smart. They know that to pay the rent and the taxes, they need customers. With dogs that need grooming.

So they get professional advice. Design a salon. Buy the necessary equipment. Then it's time to find a groomer before the big opening.

This all paints a pretty picture. Easy as 1-2-3. Once they get going, though, it's truly a bit of a wake-up call.

They soon discover, sure, it's not that hard to find a dog groomer. But what is hard? To find a GOOD groomer. They'll discover whether or not their new customers are happy with the standards.

They'll also learn that unless you time the bookings correctly, things can get chaotic. The new owners will imagine that their groomer can take care of x-many dogs per day. Because this is needed to support the business plan. And "make us rich".

Their eyes will be opened. They never realised how much actually goes into grooming. Different tools are required for different coat types. Some breeds are more complex and time-consuming than others. Blades needs to be sharpened regularly. Clippers sometimes break down. Groomers are human beings. Who also sometimes break down.

You might be among those not in the industry yet. But you imagine you'd like to open your own salon and boutique. Here is what I would do:

   * Do a grooming course. It doesn't have to be full-on 20 or 30 day course. Five days is probably sufficient. The instructor can take you through all the aspects. Explain your purpose for taking the course. Not necessarily to be the groomer. But to understand the challenges groomers contend with every day they come into work.

* When you hire a dog groomer, get help with the hiring from an experienced dog groomer. Somebody with a good reputation. You may need to pay them a few days for their help. Ideally you should book your candidates to groom under their supervision.

* Once you open, let your dog groomer talk to the customer. At least until you know what you're talking about. Don't imagine you can understand the customer requirements. And then communicate this to the dog groomer. You won't be asking the right questions. The dog groomer knows what questions to ask. He or she will know, based on the condition of the coat, what is possible. How long it will take.

Adding a degree of separation between the customer and the groomer turns into Chinese Whispers. Invariably, you'll end up with a disappointed customer. A frustrated groomer. And maybe a funny looking dog.

* What kind of cover will you have if your groomer gets ill? Or has to go away on holiday? Do you have a back-up plan? Will it hurt your business if you can't take bookings? Consider working something out with another salon. Ask for one of their staff to cover while your regular groomer is away.

* If you have a good dog groomer, treat them well. They are entitled to a fair wage. They have worked hard at their craft. They have ambitions and dreams like all of us. If you don't, you can count on them going elsewhere.

With those considerations in mind, I wish you the very best of luck. Once you get stuck in, and get more experience, you'll know a lot about dog grooming. Over time you'll be able to speak knowledgeably about this industry. About different breed standards. Coat types. Skin conditions.

And you will be bringing a fresh perspective into the industry. You won't be right all the time about the choices you make. Or the actions you take. But to be part of this industry can be fun and rewarding.

42. Grooming As Theatre

PRECIOUS: I go on a lot about the customer experience. Sometimes it's helpful to put a little bit of 'theatre' into what we do.

Let me explain. A dog owner takes their dog to the vet. The dog is there for medical reasons. The experience can be a little bit serious. People speaking softly. Being nervous or sad. Unhappy about the possible pain or suffering of their little companion.

Like vets, we are in the business of promoting good health and welfare for dogs. But we get to do it at the happy end of the spectrum. Taking the dog for grooming should be a joyful occasion. Sure, it can get a bit serious at times. Like when we come across a badly matted dog. And have to instruct the owner to come in more often.

But with a doggie spa, we can treat our customers and manage our salon in ways that are happy. Exciting. Fun. Joyful.

The theatre is an analogy I sometimes like to use. There is an expression in the theatre world about what happens 'behind the curtain'.

People go to the theatre. They witness an exciting live drama. It involves actors who have to memorise a whole bunch of lines. There are costume changes. Scene changes. Props coming in and out. Doors opening and closing.

All of these things need to be done at the precise time. Lines have to be delivered on cue. The play has to be presented seamlessly.

Behind the curtain is, literally, what happens backstage. When an actor in a play exits Stage Right, you imagine that he is off to fly to New York. Or he's off to commit a murder. Or some other intrigue.

In reality, the actor rushes down a set of stairs to a changing room. Strips off his costume. Has somebody help him into a new costume.

Stage assistants are nearby. Holding little flashlights. Watching a clock. Making sure the actor doesn't miss his next entry.

Behind the curtain you have the actors. Stage assistants. Lighting. Sound. Props. The director.

It could be complete chaos. Only by the grace of God are they able to pull off a good show. Or it could be military precision.

I think of our grooming salons along the same lines. At the 'front of house', we happily welcome our customers and their dogs. No, they aren't coming to be entertained. But the dog is coming for grooming. To be pampered. Indulged.

Our front of house should be theatre. Presentation. A good show. The customer's 'experience' must be a good one.

But in the salon, behind the curtain, it could be chaos. Either way, it shouldn't be part of the front of house experience. It shouldn't interfere with the show at Reception. So that when the customer comes to pick up, their dog is the STAR of the show. And there is no distraction of the possible noise and chaos backstage.

Watch your timings. Work efficiently. Be organised. The Show Must Go On.

43. Cats

So, as fate would have it, I'm highly allergic to cats. Which means the closest I can get to a cat is the musical in London's West End.

Although I did have a cream Persian growing up. His name was Jasper. He lived for eighteen years. And I used to show him. The allergy kicked in after I got a bit older. Anyway, it's been a while since I last groomed a cat.

That said, I still have things to say about cat grooming. Of course I do.

As with dog grooming, cats need your full and undivided attention. Even more so. If you think you need to be ahead of what a dog might do during grooming, then you REALLY need to be ahead when handling a cat.

Sure, some cats will happily sit on your table and let you do whatever needs doing. But these are the ones accustomed to regular brushing. To being kept in top condition. Other cats though will look for the nearest exit. And will stop at nothing to get out.

So, here's a few thoughts I have about grooming cats and the challenges they present. Sure, I might have learned this mostly from the side lines. But hopefully there is something here that will be of value to you. And you won't have to learn it the hard way:

* unlike dogs, cats will come to your salon in a secure cat carrier. You've heard the expression. Who let the cat out of the bag? Let a cat out its cat carrier and YOU might be in for a big surprise.

Never let the cat out of its carrier in a room that isn't completely sealed. I mean like maximum security type sealed. So don't take the cat out in the reception area. Invariably, the front door will open. And before you can say 'Nice pussy', that cat will be down the street. Or up a tree. Out of sight.

* even if the front door is secure, make sure you are in a completely closed room when taking the cat out. Maybe you've got a door that goes down to a basement. If it's left open and that cat gets away from you, it will be through that door. Down the basement. Into any of a thousand hiding places.

Not a great way to spend your day. Trying to find a cat somewhere. Hidden under a box of Star Wars collectibles. Buried deep inside a pile of old military uniforms.

* schedule your cat grooming for a time when the salon isn't busy. Ideally at a time when there aren't other dogs around. Sure, I've seen groomers handle a cat in the same salon with dogs. But you don't need to have read Dr. Seuss to know that cats and dogs sometimes don't get along. So try to avoid this. And minimise the risk of all hell breaking loose in your salon.

* it's likely you'll need two people to groom the cat if shaving is involved. One to hold the cat and move it into different positions. The other to handle the clippers.

* both groomers need to be confident with cats. You can't have a scaredy-cat groom a cat. They just scream and let go. And that doesn't help anybody.

* always cut the cat's claws first. Cats are extremely versatile with their paws. If the claws are out, look out. You could end up with some bloody racing stripes across your arms and face. But seriously, it helps prevent the cat hurting itself with its own claws if it's struggling to get away. You

can also buy some small cat shoes that go over the cat's paws. That way, any slashes to the face and you won't look like Scarface.

* don't put a safety strap around the cat's neck. Either place it around the body, under the arms. Or use a body harness instead. Connect this to a safety strap. Then to the table arm. Cats are especially good at wriggling out of things.

* if you need to shave, then I'd recommend a tight toothed clipper blade. Or a trimmer type clipper works very well.

* cats have extremely thin skin that is prone to tearing. So proceed with extreme caution.

Finally, make sure you charge your customer accordingly. If the cat isn't a problem to groom and you are happy to do it, that's great. But you have a special gift. It's hard to find a good cat groomer. So, you need to charge more. Plus, if the session required two groomers, your price will need to reflect this.

The customer won't have many options because a lot of salons don't offer cat grooming. Taking the cat to the vet, where grooming can typically involve sedation, is something the owner will want to avoid. So, if you're mad about cats, then this could be a very good opportunity.

And then, you need to find out as much as you can about Danelle German. Very important.

44. Grooming At Home

A student of mine has just converted the garage in her back yard into a salon. She is already a dog walker. And has lots of experience dog handling. She has a small ready-made list of customers. So she is excited about getting started.

If you have the space, dog grooming from your own home has its advantages. In the first place, you get to be your own boss. You don't have to travel very far to work. You don't have the overheads of commercial rent or taxes.

There are some potential down-sides. Presumably your location is in a residential area. So you don't have any footfall. You don't have a shop-front that people can see. Your signage will be limited.

Plus, you will have neighbours. They might not like dogs coming and going every day of the week.

Then, you'll have to make sure your local council will permit you to run a business from your home. Different councils have different rules. So make sure you're allowed. You really don't want the council to come knocking on your door one day. If you're not allowed, they'll close you down.

Sure, you could scramble to get all the right paperwork in place. But government doesn't move very fast. By the time you finally get permission, your customers will have gone elsewhere. You will have lost your business.

You might worry that you don't have the footfall or the shop front. I discuss this more in the Marketing section. Most of our business comes from Referrals. Word-of-mouth recommendations. So that shouldn't be a problem for a home groomer.

You'll have to think about your pricing. It's fair to say that customers would expect to pay less because you don't have a commercial premises. But don't be too swayed by this. Work out a fair price. And stick to your guns on your pricing. You are providing a much needed service. So, in my opinion, your prices don't need to be lower than the going rates.

As for your salon, design it in the same way you would a commercial salon. All the same rules about safety and hygiene and workplace efficiency.

And then give your branding a good spin. Many dog owners will prefer coming to you because they are taking their dog into a 'home'. They sometimes worry that a salon on Main Street could feel too industrial. Too commercial. That it might be too stressful for their dog. Whereas coming into a home will make their dog feel more at ease. More relaxed. Leverage this sentiment to your advantage.

As for work-life balance, there is a risk of taking your work home with you. Because you can never get away. My student is lucky because the garage is separate from the house. And it has a separate entrance. So when she closes the door behind her, that's it. She can walk across the garden and into her house. Turn on the telly. Pour herself a glass of wine. And truly unwind. Her salon is physically separate from her living premises.

Sounds like the good life.

45. Mobile Grooming

Like the groomer who works from home, running a mobile grooming business can be very liberating. No landlord. No crazy taxes for business premises. You get to choose the hours you work. You don't have to worry about opening and closing a shop at fixed hours of the day.

Mobile grooming is a fantastic way to get started. I sometimes recommend this to students of mine who dream of opening a salon. The up-front investment can be considerable. But nowhere near as much as paying a deposit on a shop space and doing it up.

Mobile grooming can range from having your own kit and grooming a dog in somebody's home. To having a fully-equipped van.

With a mobile grooming van, you drive up to the dog owner's home. Park your car in their drive or on the street. And groom the dog inside your van.

All the normal rules apply about salon safety and the health and welfare of the dog.

In terms of a business proposition, mobile grooming may just be the ticket for you. If you're able to groom six dogs in a day. Five days a week. You can earn a good living. And you get to be your own boss. You only need to build your business up to about 180 dogs. Your regulars. With the assumption that you re-book those dogs for grooming every six weeks.

Take the time to work out your business plan. And try to include a kitty for un-foreseen expenses. Getting stuck in the mud, for example. Like I did. I was having a bad week. And it got worse when I had to drive to a client outside town. In the days before Sat Nav. I got lost. Took a wrong turn. Thought I could navigate a great big mud puddle.

I wasn't able to take my mobile grooming van more than about half-way through the mud puddle. Wheels spinning. Me swearing. Van sinking deeper into the mud.

It wasn't pretty. Eventually, I gave up. I walked about a mile to the nearest house. Made a phone call. Dina, my boss, wasn't happy. A couple of hours later, the two tow-trucks eventually managed to get my van out of the mud. There wasn't much left of Dina's emergency fund though.

46. How Many Dogs

PRECIOUS: The general expectation from a salon owner is that you should be able to manage a minimum of SIX dogs in a day. All to a good standard.

Some training centres in the US won't let you 'graduate' unless you can do this.

Don't freak out if you think this is too many dogs. Perhaps you're fresh out of training. You're only confident doing three. That's fine. But now you have something to work towards. And you will get there.

When interviewing for a job, this will be one of the first questions. The employer has a business to run. They need to work out an average that they can earn from you grooming six dogs a day, five days a week. From this revenue, they need to pay your wages. The rent. The tax. The utilities. The shampoo. Business insurance. And more. After that, they might have a little bit of profit. They can take that out of the business. To pay themselves. Or put it back into the business.

So the number of dogs you are capable of grooming in a day is fundamental to being successful in a grooming career. Not just as an employee working for somebody else. But even more so if you are running your own business.

In this case, you'll find yourself trying to take on as many dogs in a day as possible. Potentially working longer and longer days. Seven days a week.

Well, that's kind of how it goes for all new businesses. Until you reach a point when you can hire somebody to share the workload.

When I say six dogs in a day, I am still including the time it takes to bathe and brush and dry. Prepping is arguably the most time consuming part.

You might be in the happy position of being a senior stylist. You rely on others – juniors - to do the prep for you. Then you just take care of the styling and scissoring. If this is the case, you should be able to complete twelve or sixteen dogs in a day.

Most of us are not in that position. So congratulations to those of you who are.

Of course all this depends on the breeds you get. A Newfoundland, for example, wouldn't count as one dog. And if you're getting wash-and-wear dogs (short hairs), many of these can be done in half the time. Less even.

Either way, you should make it a personal goal to be able to groom six dogs in a day. From start to finish. Taking responsibility for every aspect including the prep work. If you're not doing this despite years of experience, then you need to find ways to groom more efficiently.

Let's consider a simple example.

A Labradoodle, Bartholomew, has come into the salon for his groom. The coat has been slightly neglected and you will have to do a clip off. Now, before even touching the dog, some groomers will simply put that dog in the bath for its shampoo.

But what's the point of that? You're going to spend all this time shampooing and rinsing. Then shampooing and rinsing again. Then drying that long coat until the cows come home.

Why not take the clippers to Bartholomew's coat first? Before he even sees the bath?

Just do a basic clip off first. Don't worry about being even at this point. You just want to take the coat off. Then get Bartholomew into the bath. You can even out with the clippers afterwards.

This may sound logical. But, believe it or not, I recently visited a salon that insisted all dogs are washed and cleaned before using clippers on them.

That's because the salon didn't want to run their clippers through a dirty dog coat.

Yes, there is a risk of dulling the blades somewhat. So what? Get the blades sharpened.

Okay, that costs money. But not as much money as doubling or tripling the time it will take to wash and rinse and dry all that hair on the dog. It's got to come off anyway.

In our grooming we need to re-consider the way that we work currently. We need to watch some videos on YouTube. Or sign up to learn2groomdogs.com and get with the program. Look at the Resources page on my Academy website for the link.

There are a lot of great teachers out there. They will show you more efficient ways of grooming. You need to find these out. Make yourself groom more efficiently.

And here's one last piece of advice: don't be a perfectionist. Good is good enough. I speak about this at the beginning of the book. Being perfectionist will slow you down. You're working in a commercial dog grooming salon. You're not grooming the Queen's corgis.

(Unless you really are grooming the Queen's corgis. In which case, yes, take your time. Take all the time you need.)

47. Multi-Tasking

Despite what you may have heard, real men can multi-task. And I love quiche.

Where there are multiple groomers, there will be multiple dogs. Plus a system for the dogs being taken for their prepping and scissoring. It all needs to operate like clockwork. Each groomer taking turns with the bath or the dryers. Working at their stations. Focusing on their dogs.

But what if you're a solo groomer? You don't have the advantage of an assistant.

Let's say you've been booked a Westie, a Poodle and a Cocker Spaniel for 9am. And all the dogs need to be out the door by 12 noon. And they have to look good.

Sounds intense. But if you can multi-task smartly, you can do it.

First, you need to work without distraction. So put away the Blackberry or the iPhone. You can pick up those all-important facebook updates later.

Now, let's think about the dogs. The coat textures in particular. The Westie should have a wire coat. Although you'll often see them with either wire or a mix of textures.

Then you have the Poodle with a wool coat. The Poodle coat needs to be dried straight. And last, the Cocker Spaniel. Normally a silky coat. But often seen with a mix of textures.

I would start first with the Cocker. It would normally take the longest to dry. So wash and bathe and prep the Cocker first. Then use the blaster until barely damp. Place the Cocker into a crate with a towel for comfort.

You don't have to direct any heat on the dog. It should already be close to dry. Plus it's a good thing for the skin to finish drying naturally.

Now do the same with the Westie. While both dogs are in crates finishing their drying naturally, start prepping your Poodle. Remember, the Poodle has to be dried from start to finish. Once completely dried, place the dog in a clean, dry crate or kennel space.

By this time, both your Cocker and Westie should be dry. If not, just finish drying with a stand dryer with some heat if needed.

And now it's time to start styling and scissoring the first dog, the Cocker. Then the Westie. Then the Poodle.

Look at the clock. You're on your way to finishing all three dogs in three hours or less. Believe me, it's all possible. You'll have time to complete the grooming with a good finished result that will thrill each dog's owner.

On a final note - and this remains a controversial point - you can put a heat dryer on the dogs in the crates. BUT always make sure to keep a very close eye on the dogs.

And don't allow the Poodle to stay in for too long. If you haven't blast-dried correctly then once it's in the cabinet the coat will dry curly.

48. Hiring an Assistant, Bather or Prepper

Prepping a dog looks like fun. Lifting a dog into the bath. Dousing it with warm water. Lathering shampoo into its coat. It's a pretty picture. But let's be under no illusion. Prepping is hard work. And it's the most time-consuming part of the grooming process.

Good prepping is critical to successful grooming. Without a clean and thoroughly dried coat, the scissoring and styling will not be as effective.

If you are running your own salon, you should consider hiring a bather. This depends, of course, on how busy you are. But if you are booked days or weeks in advance, you are in a good position to bring in a bather. He or she can help you increase your productivity.

Perhaps your level of business doesn't justify hiring an assistant. That's fine, but it's likely that you have busy periods during the year. Like the lead-up to Christmas. There are plenty of young people who would love to come on board for a bit of work experience. Or extra pocket money.

Spend a day training them. Demonstrate the importance of deep shampooing the dog everywhere. Followed by a thorough rinse.

Ideally, you want to shampoo and rinse a dog twice. The second and final rinse needs to be extremely thorough. The dog's coat must be squeaky clean. With absolutely no trace of shampoo anywhere.

Double-check the pads to make sure there is no trace of shampoo left. Inspect the ears. The hygiene areas.

Also, make sure to demonstrate how to wash the dog's head. So that you don't get water and shampoo into the ears and the nose.

Once you are satisfied, it's time to take them through the drying and brushing out. You know how to do this yourself already. Just demonstrate and then have them take over. But there are a few key points you need to make.

1. Make sure the dog gets a good towel dry before you start the blaster. You need to reduce the amount of water on the dog as much as possible. Otherwise you're just not being efficient. Don't just use ordinary cotton towels for this. Get the super absorbent cloths. Wring them out between wiping the dog down. You'll be amazed at how much water these can remove from the coat.

2. Make sure your student understands the appropriate use of the blaster. You don't want them accidentally turning a high-powered blaster onto a tea-cup Yorkie. It won't withstand the power. It risks getting injured or seriously traumatised. Blasters should not be used on tiny dogs. Or any dog that reacts badly to the high volume of air pressure directed at them.

3. Depending on the size of the dog, you can use the blaster on a larger dog while it is still in the bath. This is a judgement call based on the layout of your salon. Sometimes it's easier to blast the dog while it's still in the bathtub. Instead of moving it to the table for blasting.

4. Follow best practise for drying and brushing out. Move section by section over the dog.

Back. Middle. Front. Head. Tail.

5. Make absolutely sure that the dog is dry dry dry before being handed over to you for scissoring.

Depending on the level of skill of your prepper / assistant, you may be able to get them trimming the hair in-between the pads. And clipping the dog's nails.

You can increase your productivity radically by focusing on the part of your job that requires real skill and experience. Assign the more time-consuming, but simpler, tasks to your less-skilled helper.

You won't be short of people begging to help you out. Whether just for the experience. Or to earn a little bit of extra holiday money. You'll find your business operating more efficiently. More profitably. Because you've been able to take on additional bookings without taking on much additional overhead.

49. Hiring Someone 'Different'

Here's a subject close to my heart. I was once invited to judge a competition. But the woman organising asked me, in hushed tones, to lose my Mohawk. And remove my piercing.

I was younger then. I'm not as hip or stylish any longer. As Precious likes to remind me. But I was taken aback. Here I was, having won all kinds of competitions. Then, being asked to alter my appearance. To appease a certain expectation. An expectation that I should look 'normal'.

But I ask, what is 'normal'? It's disappointing that many of us still feel we need 'to conform'.

The same applies if you need to hire a groomer. You'll meet a number of candidates. They will be eager to please. For the most part, they'll have a conservative appearance. Because 'most' people do.

So I often hear from other groomers, former students, for example. They tell me they didn't get a job at such-and-such salon. And I'm stunned. Because I'll know this groomer to have won competitions. To be extremely good at what they do. They're passionate. Talented.

They might have piercings. Or crazy hair colours. Or outrageous dress sense. But this intrigues me. This is somebody who is willing to live creatively. Somebody who cuts through life without needing everybody's approval.

At the risk of using psycho-babble, these groomers dare to be different. I think it's a good thing they're not 'ordinary'. I am not excited by ordinary. I am not interested in the conventional. It's 'boredinary' (bored + ordinary). I want my business to be extraordinary. If you're slightly out of your comfort zone with the groomer's appearance, think of it as an opportunity. At least give him or her a chance to showcase their skills.

I'm not saying you should look more favourably at a scruffy candidate. Like they've just had a long hard night partying. This is altogether different. I am simply suggesting you keep an open mind.

A lot of dog groomers are very creative people. This could be expressed in the way they look. But they could also be a complete natural with a pair of scissors. You don't want to miss out because you dismissed them for their non-conventional dress sense.

50. Incentives For Employees

If you run a grooming salon, it means you need to manage employees. This means running a tight schedule of the hours they work. Paying them promptly. Taking care of the administration to do with their taxes or national insurance.

But an employee needs more than that. They need to enjoy the workplace atmosphere. They need to be treated with respect for the good work they do. They need to be rewarded for the value they add to your business.

So, in addition to a competitive wage, you have to come up with meaningful ways of keeping them motivated. Generally, this means creating opportunities for them to earn a little bit of extra money on top of their wages. It isn't always about money of course. There are other ways of recognising your employee's contribution to the business that provide satisfaction in their job.

Here are a few examples of things I've done in the past to keep my groomers and assistants happy:

* Allow your groomers to keep the takings for walk-in clients who want their dog's nails clipped. If you have multiple employees, let them take turns at doing a dog's nails.

* If you don't have retail in your shop, allow the groomer – or groomers – to sell certain retail items. Like shampoos. Brushes. Doggie cologne. Or even dog treats. A lot of hairdressers work this way. They shampoo their client's hair with a certain brand. Then sell the shampoo to their client for a percentage commission of the retail price.

* Depending on the number of employees you have, consider running an 'employee of the month' contest. This needs to be fun and light-hearted. But the reward might be their image in a frame at the front of the shop.

* Perhaps you offer an at-home boarding service and you have a groomer who is able to provide this. You still need to have the insurance in place as a business. But you would share the revenue with your employee. A typical rate for this is 60-40 in the employee's favour.

* Like the at-home boarding service, you could offer a cat-sitting service to local residents. You could offer your employees the opportunity to take care of the cat-sitting. Again, this needs to be on a revenue-share basis. Like the dog boarding. Because your business has to cover the insurance. For both boarding and cat-sitting, make sure you have a proper customer registration form that includes a waiver the customer needs to sign. Do this in order to reduce your liability if something goes horribly wrong.

* Run occasional contests. If your groomers help cover retail sales, then offer a reward for most sales generated in a month. The reward could be something like dinner for two at a local restaurant.

I'm sure you can come up with loads of other ideas. The point of this is simply to recognise that your employees are human. They need to be respected and rewarded for their good work. Provide them the opportunity to earn a little extra. Keep the atmosphere in the salon fun with a little bit of friendly competition from time to time. Also, if they are earning extra money, make sure they understand their responsibility reporting the extra income.

51. Adding Retail to Your Grooming

When we dream of starting our own salon, we may have in mind a wonderful salon along with a wonderful boutique. With lots of products at the front. If the customer has to come here with their dog anyway, then maybe I can provide their dog's essentials.

I am in the perfect position to sell them the right shampoo. Or flea medication. Or exactly the right kind of food that will improve the health of their skin and coat.

Yep, sure. It's a nice image.

But retail is challenging. Hugely time-consuming. And must be approached with extreme caution.
If you are a solo groomer, forget it. Unless you really know what you're doing.

I'm talking about the dog groomer who wants to go into business with another groomer. A friend. Or a sister. The scenario is a dog grooming salon in the back. Retail boutique at the front reception area.

You work in the 'trade'. So you can set up an account with a pet supply wholesaler. They will happily sell you products at a wholesale price. Which you then sell to your customer at a retail price. You keep the difference. This is called your Gross Profit.

Your 'Net Profit' - the amount of money you actually get to put in your pocket and take home with you (this is your 'income' so you still get taxed on it) – is your Gross Profit less (minus) any additional expenses it takes to get that product to the customer. Like your rent and wages.

Here's an example. If you're selling a bag of food to a customer, the Gross Profit margin will be about 20 per cent. So, for a bag of food that the customer buys for £10, your Gross Profit is about £ 2.

Okay, so let's say you sell ten bags of food in a day. That's an extra £20 Gross Profit in a day. Doesn't sound that difficult. Or that much. But six days a week and you're looking at £120. In a month, that could make a difference of almost £500 Gross Profit.

Maybe that pays the rent. Contributes to the wages. Great.

And then there are your other products.

Let's say you've got toys and treats. Beds. Medication. Cat litter. Shampoos. Collars and leads. Let's assume there is at least a forty per cent Gross Profit margin on these products. There could be less, there could be more. It varies. But generally you need about 40 per cent for the products that are not dog food. Dog treats may have a better margin. Don't think of these in the same category as dog food.

At minimum, you should be able to sell the same amount in value of these products as the dog food. So, in a day, let's say you sell £100 of dog food. Then you should expect to sell £100 worth of the non-dog food products (collars, leads, shampoo etc).

This is just a rough sketch, remember. It all depends on how you develop your business. If you're in a good area with lots of footfall (passing trade) and enthusiastic customers, you could do very well.

It's one customer at a time. And pretty soon your retail is covering all the rent and the wages for any staff. This doesn't include any online sales you might be making. Which is a whole other opportunity to exploit.

So what are the challenging bits? First, your retail will require significant up-front investment. It is hugely time-consuming to research and learn all the products. It takes time each week to re-order and re-stock.

Fine, that's all part of the program. And it can be a lot of fun to talk knowledgeably about dog products. To have your finger on the pulse of what is going on in the industry.

But I have a warning. Don't allow yourself to become a slave to your retail at the expense of your grooming. You might need to combine your grooming and retail revenue to make your business plan work. But be warned: there will be times when you spend twenty minutes talking to somebody about the health benefits of a type of food. You could have spent that time scissoring a dog. And you could end up resenting your retail side of the business. So make sure you've got somebody to share the workload with you.

And then get clever about it. Leverage your expertise as a dog groomer to select and recommend products with a good margin.

For example, apply the finishing spritz of cologne on the dog when your customer comes to collect their dog after grooming.

Or encourage them to buy a bottle of the wonderful shampoo that you use in your salon.

Tailor your retail to the types of dogs that come to you for grooming. It doesn't make sense to have chunky masculine dog collars suited to Labradors and hunting dogs if you are grooming Miniature Poodles and Bischon Frisés.

And sell lots of treats. These usually have a good margin and they make for a good impulse purchase.

52. Other Business Opportunities

I have worked in a lot of exciting places. I've always been intrigued by the range of products and services in our industry. The inventive things that salon owners do to differentiate their business. To create additional revenue streams.

Your grooming could be your main thing. But it's also a great platform from which to create other opportunities. Because what you have is a LIST of customers. They come to you for grooming. But they spend money on their pets in other ways too.

You can use that list as a platform to offer additional services. Like my section on retail, don't do this at the expense of your grooming. But if you've got somebody to share the workload with you, then there are some cool opportunities.

Yes, retail is the natural bedfellow for a salon. Same with add-on services like dog walking. Daycare. Boarding. Cat-sitting.

Other opportunities I've seen include the following. Not everything works. It depends on how well you execute the idea. How well your customers respond to it.

Pet Photography – if you have a good eye, you could consider taking pet portraits. You have the skills to groom a dog wonderfully. To make them picture perfect. You have space in your salon. So maybe you could rig a backdrop. Some lighting. Take pictures. Sell the digital image to your customer. Or use a printing service to provide your customer with a lovely portrait.

Painted pet portraits – there are many artists who paint pet portraits. Ask the artist to provide a couple of samples. Put these on display. Agree a percentage commission for every portrait ordered through you.

Dog bakery – learn some recipes for dog treats. Bake at home. Sell to your customers. Try to get regular orders. Perhaps approach other pet shops or dog-friendly venues in your city. They might be willing to take a batch on a weekly basis. Sell to them at a wholesale price.

Dog parties – host or manage dog parties on your premises. It takes time and organisation. But if you have the space, then your premises are a natural fit. Tell your customers about it. Some of them will absolutely love you for it. Because there aren't a lot of places you can do this sort of thing. Dog owners are happy to have one or two dogs at home. But not ten or more. So they can have the party at your place. It's great fun for families and children to participate in a dog party. You provide the premises. The dog treats. Decorations. A dog birthday cake. You get to be an event manager. Your customer pays you an overall charge. And you keep a nice margin after expenses.

Sale or Return – if you do retail, you'll get occasional requests from people asking to sell their products in your store. I don't mean the normal suppliers. I mean the sister of a customer who knits doggy jumpers (sweaters). Or the local carpenter who creates little wooden puzzles for dogs. If you like what they do, take their products. But do it on a Sale or Return basis. Anytime something sells through your shop, you get an agreed share of the money. If the items don't sell after a couple of months, just return them. If you're open minded about these things, you might accidentally happen onto something that sells really well.

Creative grooming – take a course in creative grooming. Or Japanese style grooming. Become really good at it. Offer it to your customers. Become an expert. Hold a workshop for other groomers.

Hardly a day goes by without hearing about some new fad in the pet industry. Doggie Yoga. Interactive games that cats can play on an iPad. There isn't a shortage of new ideas out there. New ways of making money. You can leverage your customer list. Use it as a platform to help you sustain a living in a field you love.

53. Pick-Up & Drop-Off

COLIN: I've been called a lot of things. One of them is Nervous Nelly.

It was my assistant. I had to keep reminding her to call the customers. To let them know that their dog was ready.

"But the dog is still on the table," she would say.

"Yes," I would answer. Trying not to glower. "But by the time they get in their car. Find a parking spot. Walk into the shop. That dog will be ready to go."

"You're such a Nervous Nelly."

I know what she meant. I don't like to have dogs hanging about in the salon unnecessarily.

Because a dog in my care is a dog that I have to worry about. The salon is safe. Secure. Comfortable. The other dogs are well-socialised. They have access to water. Everything is under control.

But I still don't like it.

I try to minimise the time a dog is in my care. That the dog is my responsibility. Because I'm a worrier.

It sounds counter-intuitive.

Why work with dogs if I don't like the responsibility – the worry – of having dogs in my care?

Well, because I love dogs. And I love doing good things for them. But I want them to go home. And be safe with their owners. As soon as possible.

Which makes me reluctant to do those additional things. Like adding dog walking to my business. Or day-care. Pick-up and drop-off.

I worry too much.

PRECIOUS: Colin, I've never known you to be so WET. Dry off. Live a little. The fact is, I'd rather have a worrier look after my dog than a non-worrier.

Because a worrier doesn't get complacent. A worrier won't be nonchalant about letting a dog out of his sight.

Colin, if you were to add pick-up and drop-off to your business, I know what you would do.

You'd get a really good car. Not just any car. A car that is properly equipped to transport dogs safely. Securely.

You'd get the maximum amount of insurance possible. Because if anything ever went wrong – and it takes just a split second – you'd be covered. If a dog were hurt, or killed, in your care, the owners would investigate. And they'd seek compensation. You wouldn't risk your business without proper cover.

And you wouldn't trust just anybody with dog walks or pick-up and drop-off. You would have to be 100 per cent convinced this was somebody totally reliable.

Having dogs in our care is a HUGE responsibility.

So, if YOU, dear reader, want to add pick-up and drop-off to your business, go for it. But be a worrier about it. Like Colin. Never get carefree about handling dogs in your care.

Come to terms with this realisation first. And then think about the benefits for your business.

You will attract new customers. Often these are older people who are less mobile. They can't drive anymore. Or don't have the support to take their dog for grooming.

Charge a fixed fee on top of the grooming. You'll have to limit the pick-up and drop-off to a specific geographic area though. You don't want to lose half a day trundling across town to collect just one dog.

Look, there are many businesses that provide pick-up and drop-off. Pet taxis. Kennels. They do it happily. Without incident.

You don't have to exaggerate the risks. The negative consequences. But you do have to keep in mind that you increase your risk. You might be comfortable with that. But it can be a good thing to be a bit of a worrier about it.

54. Creative Grooming

PRECIOUS: Have you seen the images yet? Of Poodles. Labradoodles. Or Cockerpoos. Looking like Pandas. Tigers. Or clowns? Get on Google now. Creative Grooming is going wild. Literally.

We don't see this in London very much at all. But it's happening with fantastic results in places across the US. And especially in Hong Kong and Tokyo.

There was a report in the news the other day. A Labradoodle shaved to look like a lion. Somewhere in SmallTown, USA. It sure gave the local residents a scare.

Maybe it's a clip or colouring to make a dog look like another animal. A pawdicure with painted nails. Or a dog that now looks like a Teenage Mutant Ninja Turtle.

There is no shortage of criticism for so-called Creative Grooming. The results can be shocking. Laughable. Fantastic. Offensive. Outrageous.

I'm with Colin on this one. Our dogs are our friends. We must treat them with Dignity. With reverence. That means we should be laughing WITH them. Not AT them.

Creative Grooming can be wonderful fun. Whether it's a splash of colour here and there. Or a complete transformation into Winnie the Pooh's Tigger.

Of course there are critics. The nay-sayers who worry that the colouring causes harm. Or encourages DIY jobs at home by amateurs. Which may lead to devastating consequences.

By all means, it should only be done by trained professionals. Using safe, pet-friendly non-toxic colours. For example, nail polish. Dogs lick their paws. So we have to use pet-friendly nail polish. Not the human stuff.

I wouldn't get too worried about the kill-joys. As long as we don't ridicule our respected companions it can be a lot of fun. Not just for us. The dogs too.

A friend recently walked her dyed-blue Standard Poodle down Oxford Street. It's a main shopping area in London. The dog got so much attention. It was all favourable and positive. It wasn't stressful for the dog. She just lapped it up in her stride. Like she was a celebrity on the red carpet.

We just need to be mindful the attention isn't overwhelming. If the dog is getting stressed by it, then that's enough. Take a break before the next celebrity appearance.

Stencil colouring is also worth considering. Especially for Xmas or Hallowe'en. Or the 4th of July. You can get these little blow-pen kits that come with stencils. Create the shape of Santa Claus on top of the dog's back. Or the Stars and Stripes. It's safe. Cute. Harmless.

Creative colouring could add value to your business. Maybe attract a little bit of free media attention. Newspapers always need to fill their pages. What better than a piece about your salon transforming a Cockerpoo into a Panda bear?

Just make sure it's done professionally. With pet-friendly products. And that the dog is always a happy and willing accomplice.

55. Taking Customer Details

PRECIOUS: If there's one thing I like, it's organisation. With a capital B. Call me what you will. But I insist on things being just so. I like my scissors to sit neatly in their own little cases. For towels to be stacked with the folded edges aligned. Shampoo bottles on the shelf in a perfect row. With the labels symmetric.

That's how I like things in the salon.

When it comes to Reception, same applies. I need to have my customer details immediately to hand. In the old days, I used recipe cards. Then I upgraded to an Excel spread-sheet. Now I use Customer Relationship Management software (CRM). It's not fancy. But it does the trick.

I am particular about customer details. I like to get the following information:

Dog's name (I arrange everything by the dog's name).
Dog breed – which I select from a drop-down list. Or enter manually.
Customer first name. Last name.
Customer mobile number.
A second telephone number.
Email address.
Phsyical address.
Dog's birthday.
Appointments.
Vet's contact details.

Then I have a text-field for notes. About the dog. Or about the customer. For example, "4FR" – which means I used a 4F blade. With a reverse clip.

But the text field is useful for other information. For example, the dog only uses medicated shampoo. Has an ear infection. Or the customer needs to pay in advance.

I have added little tick-boxes for my Blacklist and Whitelist.

And that's about it.

With this information, I send customers text message or email reminders.

And every morning I filter the customer list based on the dog's birthday. If it's the dog's birthday, I send a happy birthday email, using a ready-made template. My customers love it.

All of this I can do cost-effectively. There are excellent cheap programs that you can find online. They might originally be designed for a hairdresser. Or a restaurant. But I was able to find a system and tweak it for my purposes.

I spent a lot of money on my point-of-sale system for the retail part of my shop. Which is all very slick. And, I have to say, has been worth it. But I didn't spend much money on my booking system. Which I'm glad about.

I still use a proper appointments book though. When a customer calls to book their dog, I ask the dog's name, and breed. And I always answer with a smile. A great big lipstick smile. Even if I'm annoyed with Colin.

Then I slide over to my computer. Punch in the dog's name.

I've got the customer information almost immediately. So then I can start talking to the customer using their first name. Often, I'll recognise the customer anyway.

I can see when they last came into the salon. I can see if we need to be aware of anything before booking them in.

I find an available time-slot in the appointments book. Next to it, I write down the dog's name first. Then the breed. The customer's first name. Their mobile number. And I put a little star next to the appointment if the notes on the computer need to be consulted.

As you can imagine, my hand-writing is impeccable. I used to win penmanship awards in school. Because I'm like that.

But often I'm too busy grooming to take bookings. So it's usually Colin. Or one of our assistants.

I love Colin. You know I do. But, invariably, he doesn't get it right. The writing is illegible. Or the telephone number is incorrect.

How hard can it be? That's when my bossy side comes out. I have a tantrum. A hysterical fit. I once threw the book at him. It hit him in the face. And knocked out a front tooth. I felt terrible.

I'm sure I'm not alone on this one, though. I imagine these tantrums are taking place up and down the country every day. In grooming salons. Hair-dressers. Restaurants. Anywhere that relies on having to read somebody else's hand-writing.

Maybe it's not worth the aggravation any longer. And I certainly don't condone violence in the work-place. Maybe I'll invest in a fully computerised system. Sooner, rather than later. To preserve my sanity. And Colin's teeth.

56. Slow Days in the Salon

Some days are so slow. The phone doesn't ring. Cobwebs are forming on the front door. You don't have any dogs on the table. You've scrubbed the bath three times. You needed something to do.

You think it's just a lull. It's that time of year. People are on holidays. I'll be busy again once they're back. Or you're in one of those in-between-y type months. Like November. You suspect people are waiting until closer to Christmas.

You have faith that this is just a hump. You'll be busy again. Or you're terrified. Because you're not sure how to cover the rent. Or wages. Or other bills. It shouldn't be this way. Even at times when people say "it's quiet everywhere". Poppycock.

You need to design your bookings for regular grooming. So that you don't have days without any dogs. Principally, this comes down to re-booking. Re-book your customers before they leave your salon.

If they worry that they'll forget, reassure them. You'll send them a reminder in the week or days before grooming. A text message. Or a phone call. Plus, you can fill in the details on an appointment card.

To keep a coat in optimum condition, you need to see the dog every four to six weeks. If the owner isn't brushing their dog at home, it might be more often than that.

You might also like to find out if the dog sleeps in bed with them. I've heard that three out of five dogs in the UK enjoy this privilege. In which case, suggest the dog come in for a weekly or bi-weekly bath. Or have the dog bathed every time the owners change their bed linen.

And those customers who don't re-book? Prompt them in a few weeks with a reminder. We have busy lives, right? So do our customers. They have all kinds of things to distract them. Sometimes they forget to book their dog. But what if they received a text message from you? A polite reminder?

My vet uses text messaging very effectively. I get reminded every three months that it's time for Jigsaw's Flea Treatment. I like being reminded. It doesn't feel like the vet is 'selling' anything to me. Of course she is. Because she needs to earn a living. Like the rest of us. But keeping Jigsaw healthy with a reminder is actually a service. It benefits Jigsaw and me.

The same applies with grooming. Regular visits to the grooming salon are good for our dogs' health and well-being.

Make that your mind-set. Be led by the conviction that grooming is good and necessary. Don't be led by the worry that you are being pushy. Or sales-y.

Educate your customers about the importance of grooming. You know it. They should know it. So when they get a text from you four or six weeks after Buffy's last visit, they'll see it as a service. A gentle reminder.

So, if you're playing a long game of Monopoly with your assistant, stop. Do not pass Go. It's time to get on the phone. Send some text messages. Make phone calls.

Look back eight weeks into your appointments book. Contact everybody who hasn't come back since. Send them a nice message. Remind them that Buffy is due her next grooming appointment. That you look forward to seeing her again. And get these dogs coming back on a regular basis.

57. Website

Years ago the Yellow Pages would be delivered to our front doors. Depending on where you lived, these could be the size and weight of a large brick. But have you noticed how thin the Yellow Pages printed editions are these days?

The Internet has changed things radically. Now all you hear is 'Google it'. And that's how some of your customers will find you. Mobile applications like Yelp are starting to make a difference too.

It is critical therefore that you have a website. And it's helpful that you list it with a few free online directories.

There are different types of websites you can have. For example, a simple brochure site. Doesn't do much. Just has some nice images and descriptions of your business. But little or no interaction.

Or you may have a fully e-commerce enabled website with all the bells and whistles. The ability for customers to purchase a range of products. Sign up for newsletters. Request bookings. Bake cookies. And more.

Whatever you have, you'll have a section about your grooming. So I'd suggest the following:

* try to use as many pictures as possible. A picture tells a thousand words. Don't use stock photographs. Use your own. They don't need to be perfect, professionally shot and lit images. The pictures I take on my iphone provide authenticity. These are perfectly acceptable.

* include some before and after shots. Include some images of dogs in the bath. With suds everywhere. These can be fun and cute.

* make sure you get written permission from customers to use images of their dogs. You'll need the customer to sign a property release. You can find examples of these on the web. Just Google 'Property Release'.

* try to include some videos on your site. Like your images, these don't need to be professional productions. Just amateur videos that give people a nice impression of you. Who you are. How much you love your job. How well you take care of their cherished companions. Happy customers telling the camera how much they love you.

* avoid too much text. Keep your sentences short. To the point. Easy to read. Your website is not the place for you to publish the Great American Novel.

* mention the benefits of grooming to a dog's health and wellbeing. It isn't just haircuts.

* provide a description of the shampoos or treatments you use. Take pride in having selected only the finest of products. Make sure you are using shampoos you actually believe in.

* identify what makes you stand out from other groomers. If you offer additional services or special treatments, mention this. For example, "we are the first salon in the West End to offer the oatmeal and honey facial scrub."

* add logos of any professional bodies you belong to. Advertise any certifications. Qualifications. Or awards you've earned.

When it comes to pricing, I recommend only providing pricing guidance on your website. As we know, dogs come in all shapes and sizes. With their coats in all conditions. Prices will vary. Provide an approximate price instead of a fixed price. You want to compel people to call you. To chat about what's involved. How long it will take. What price they can expect to pay. Then use your formidable charm to book them in.

On your website, provide a description of what's included in a full groom (or 'spa treatment').

For example:

* General health check - inspecting the condition of the coat and skin and dog's general well-being
* Clipping the nails
* Treating the ears
* Two warm water baths
* Fluff-dry
* Styling to breed standards
* Refreshing finishing spritz

I've kept this simple. You can elaborate as you like. Get descriptive with your offering. Purple your prose.

Internet Marketing is a whole other ball game. Whole series of books are written on the subject. It's something I hear people talk about. They say things like Google rankings and Search Engine Optimisation. Back-links. Keywords. YouTube videos and social media.

Having a website is all fine and dandy. But you still need people to find your website. So it's worth paying some attention to these things.

But be careful.

The Internet is ideal for companies that want to reach a really wide audience. Like worldwide. If you run a grooming salon, you're serving more of a local market. You want to be found on Google. But you don't need a hugely expensive corporate website. And you don't have to invest very much money – if any at all – with online directories.

They may promise you increased traffic to your website. They will say that a few conversions (new customers) will justify your monthly fee. They can be very convincing. Showing you all kinds of metrics. Demonstrating how your business will stand out from others.

That's fine. But you're a dog grooming salon. Not a restaurant. Nightclub. Jeweller. Or international handbag distributor.

The risk is that you sign up to a substantial on-going monthly charge. I'm not convinced it's worth it. You're a local business. You serve a local community. Your customers will come from the local area. Only a handful of enthusiasts will travel across town, totally out of their way, avoiding their own local groomers, to come to you.

58. Advertising & Marketing

Leaflets in the local area. A small ad in a local magazine from time to time. Putting up posters in other nearby shops.

Holding the occasional event in a local park is also good. A family-friendly fun dog show. Agility demonstration. Dog bakery bake sale. You could invite local media to attend. They always need copy to fill their pages.

These things are helpful at raising awareness in your local community. And don't cost much.

In my experience, the single best source for generating business is Referrals. Word-of-mouth.

Your grooming is your own best advertising. A nicely groomed dog will get lots of attention when it's playing in the park. Or out for a walk. Other dog owners will ask them where they go. The owners will recommend you.

The 80-20 rule applies. Eighty per cent of my business comes from 20 per cent of my customers recommending me. With that, I can't resist a little plug here for Learn2GroomDogs.com. Melissa provides a really good lecture on the four Rs: Referrals, Rebooking and Retention Rate.

We have an advantage. Dogs go for walks. They become little walking advertisements of our services. So groom your dogs well. Make sure you re-book your customers. And serve your customers with a smile. Make it a great experience for them. So that they want to come back to you. And tell all their friends - and all the other dog owners they meet – about you.

Save your money on all the fancy-pants super SEO-type programs and directories. Instead of Search Engine Optimisation, work on your Grooming Optimisation.

59. Pricing

If you haven't done it, I'll bet you've been tempted.

RING RING.

"Hello. I have a Poodle and a Westie and a Cocker. How much do you charge?"

Puh-leez.

This is the oldest trick in the book. Price-calling other salons. It's not very cool. And it kind of makes all us groomers suspicious of each other.

Yes, you should have a general idea of what other salons are charging. Of course you can take a look at some websites. They may have some pricing guidance posted.

So you'll need to be in the general ball-park to be competitive.

Keep that in mind. But work out your own pricing.

I sometimes find it helpful to start with an hourly 'guide' price. So, FOR EXAMPLE ONLY, let's say £30 per hour. Per groomer. I make bookings with the assumption that a medium size dog will generally take 1.5 hours. So my 'guide' price for an average (medium) size dog would be £45.

This assumes that the groomer can comfortably manage SIX dogs in an eight-hour day. Including time for lunch and coffee breaks.

So, if that's my 'median' price for a 'medium' dog, I adjust the scale for small dogs. Large dogs. Extra large dogs.

I then work out a rate for just a bath and dry. A higher rate for scissoring / styling. Another rate for a shave-off. And a separate rate for hand-stripping.

It's tricky to do my pricing based simply on breeds. Because there can a lot of difference – eg. a small Yorkie versus a big Yorkie. So my pricing will have to vary, usually on the basis of size. The time and effort involved.

I always make sure I have a minimum. Doesn't matter what breed. Or how small. If the customer has made a booking, there will be a minimum charge. I might use £30 per hour as my guidance pricing.
But my minimum will be £35. So that's what I'll charge. Even if it only took an hour to groom the dog.

When I speak at grooming events, there is usually a Question and Answer session. The question always comes up about pricing. I always warn groomers not to go cheap. Your customers won't value your services. Don't be afraid to bump up your prices. Or even be a bit pricey. A lot of skill and training goes into grooming dogs. Our pricing needs to reflect this.

60. Smooth Coats

Wouldn't it be wonderful if every dog that came for grooming was smooth coated and we could get the dog bathed, dried and brushed inside 30 minutes from start to finish?

Well, no, of course not. We'd all be bored to tears. Many of us would never have gone into grooming in the first place. There would be no creative element. No craft.

Dog owners are becoming more aware of the benefits of regular grooming. It's not just about stylish haircuts or pom poms for Poodles. The owners of Staffies, Bulldogs, Dalmatians, even Great Danes, are booking appointments. These smooth coats are sometimes described by us groomers as 'wash and wear' dogs.

And getting them into the salon on a regular basis can be a very good thing. Not just for the dog, but for your grooming business.

First of all, you will provide a good vigorous shampoo of the dog which is good for their skin and coat. You'll run a de-shedder over the dog before or after the bath. Do the nails. Clean the ears. All of this is good for the dog's health and well-being.

Second, you won't be losing time drying and brushing out a long coat. So you should be able to complete the grooming easily inside an hour. Maybe even 30 minutes. Your book might already be full for the day. But I would encourage you to fit the dog in. For those customers that need the dog groomed immediately. You'll just have to multi-task a little more effectively. But it's a handy little bump of extra money into your business to fit them in.

61. Big Dogs & Little Dogs

A friend of mine once ran a salon that, geographically, was located between two very different neighbourhoods. One community was smart and upmarket. The other area was less 'salubrious', as they say.

The dogs from the upmarket area were all your little white Malteses and Bischons and Poodle mixes. The dogs from the other neighbourhood were big, muscular dogs. Staffordshire Bull Terriers. Pitbulls. Rottweillers. The owners were equally muscular.

She wanted to attract the upmarket customers because she also wanted to develop her retail. She wanted her retail to cater to the cute end of dogs. So she sold prams and designer pet carriers. Tiny outfits. Little necklaces. Doggie pawfume. Bling collars. Diamante everywhere.

It was a lovely shop. Clean. Sparkling. Swish. With her grooming she introduced an organic facial scrub. She offered Dead Sea Mud Bath Treatment. She installed a little water fountain at the entrance. Surrounded it with great big potted palm trees. It was a divine little spa for little dogs.

But then, the owners of the big, muscular dogs also wanted their dogs groomed. Makes sense. Most of them were short-haired (the dogs). But, you know, they still need a good shampoo and brush out. Nail clipping. Ear cleaning. She's a dog lover. So of course she would happily book these dogs for a 'spa'.

But there was a problem. Her customers from 'uptown' – the customers that she wanted to cater to – didn't like 'sharing' her shop with the customers from the other area. Their worry was that their precious little white dog might get eaten by one of the big muscular dogs.

How could she reconcile the two types of customers? She ended up devising a system of taking short-haired dogs for grooming only on certain days of the week. This worked to some extent. But she was still in a tricky position.

A customer would take their tiny Chihuahua to a salon for grooming. Then get alarmed if they saw a big dog in the salon. It's not that the big dogs are unfriendly. It's just that they're big. And her little dog is, well, little. Even just playing, the big dog could accidentally hurt the little dog.

I know groomers who get very specific about the dogs they are willing to groom. They will flatly refuse to groom dogs that don't fit the image of their salon. But we're into this because we're dog lovers, right? It seems unfair to say no to any dog. Plus you get lots of lovely owners of these dogs. Why should they be penalised? It almost smacks of prejudice. Or doggy racism.

My friend made it work. She got smart with her bookings. She built up a regular clientele from both neighbourhoods. Offering incentives to come on certain days of the week. In the end, it didn't become as segregated as she initially feared it might.

Saturdays were a complete mix of little dogs and big dogs. And their respective dog owners. Young men in track-suits. Mixing with divorcees in pearls. Maybe there was something else going on that she didn't anticipate.

If nothing else, all I can say is that you need to be smart about choosing your location. If you want to cater to a specific market, or niche, make sure you've got the right location.

62. Nearby Competitor

PRECIOUS: Dog grooming salons aren't like coffee shops. One coffee shop opens up across the street from another. It benefits both shops. Because it helps create a 'trendy' area.

But if a new pet parlour opened up near me? It would drive me mental. I've done all this work to create a great reputation. I've got lots of loyal, happy customers. And now I have to deal with a competitor.

Customers can be fickle. They like bright, shiny new objects. Some of them may rush over to my competitor. Try them out.

I know this. Because I'm like that. A new brand of scissors comes along. I'm there trying them on for size. Oohing and Aahing.

But a new pet parlour? In MY neighbourhood?

I'd be tempted to slash my prices. Wait them out. See who blinks first.

But that could be a path of mutually assured destruction.

It's a risk I can't take.

I'll have to innovate. I'll have to come up with something new and exciting. Offer new treatments that set 'me' apart from 'them'. Work my list of customers.

I'll have to be more pro-active about re-booking customers. Get them in the diary. Call the customers I haven't seen for a while. Remind them that their dog is overdue its grooming.

I could re-vamp my loyalty program. Create a compelling offer my customers can't refuse. Offer free nail-clipping for my regulars. Or a £5 tidy-up in between grooming appointments.

I could also visit my new competition. Say hello. Introduce myself. Welcome them to the neighbourhood.

A bit of competition can be a good thing. It's healthy for us as a business. It keeps us progressing in our careers. Coming up with new offers. Providing new services. Upping our game. It prevents us from getting complacent.

In fact, maybe there's an opportunity. There may come a time when you actually recommend somebody to your competition. Or the other way around.

For example, maybe you don't like grooming cats. And they do. You can send cat customers to them. Maybe they don't offer hand-stripping. But you do. They can send hand-stripping customers to you.

Sure, it might be idealistic. But I've recently seen this with some friends. They have a salon. A nearby competitor opened. Fortunately, there are enough dogs in the area that they can both do well.

Instead of trying to destroy each other, they co-operate.

Each salon has a retail shop attached. They actually take turns going to the wholesaler and buying supplies. When one of the shops runs low on something, they call the other. They help each other out this way.

And, strange as it may sound, they occasionally go for drinks together. They compare notes about certain known problem customers.

Stuck with lemons, they made lemonade.

Trust me. I wouldn't like it if somebody new came along and opened up nearby.

But whatever the outcome, it's important to stay professional. Who knows what the future will hold for either of you? Yes, I'm idealistic. I want us groomers to stick together. Not to resent each other. Or get paranoid that the other guy is out to ruin us.

63. Seasonal Ideas

PRECIOUS: Hello everyone! Don't you just love Christmas? That season of good cheer. With lots of sparkling lights in the cool, dark, snowy nights. Everybody being really nice to everybody else. Especially in the car parking lot outside the shopping mall.

Unless you live in Australia, of course. Where the conditions are more summery. You won't be roasting chestnuts on an open fire. You'll be enjoying a little cocktail next to the barbecue. Either way, whatever the occasion, this is a chance for you to dress up your shop with a holiday theme.

And we all love dressing up. Especially Colin.

And there are plenty of occasions in the year. Make your shop 'spooky' if it's Hallowe'en. Or full of LOVE, if it's Valentines. Bunny rabbits and Easter eggs if it's, uhm, Easter.

You can also add holiday-themed bows and bandanas to your dogs. Or explore a bit of creative colouring. More about that in a second.

First, let's look at grooming bows. Remember years ago as children when we would do 'crafts' at school? At home? Or in summer camp?

Have you ever sat down with a ribbon and created a bow from it? Well, if you find that sort of thing fun and relaxing, then read on.

Colin loves it. He might be a scissor-hands when it comes to styling a Poodle. But when it comes to making bows he is all thumbs.

It's both painful and entertaining to watch Colin attempt this. But he thinks he's good at it. I just sort of cringe. But I re-assure him that yes, Colin, your bows are beautiful.

As soon as his back is turned though, I race to the computer. I get on ebay and search for dog grooming bows. You'll find a lot of options. Many of them in bright and wonderful festive colours. Or holiday themes. Usually at a very good price.

So this is how it works. After you have finished grooming the dog, fasten the bow (make sure it isn't an over-sized bow) to the D-ring on the collar. Where the lead gets attached.

I'd recommend NOT tying the bow to the dog's ears (this can pinch the skin and restrict the blood flow – which can have nasty consequences).

Try to pick a colour or style of bow that compliments the dog's colour. You'll be surprised how enthusiastic customers can get. Some owners even collect the bows. Don't mock. They love their dog. And you have made them feel special.

When the dog and its owner are out and about, the bows become a talking point. Naturally, the owners will mention that their dog went to you. Which is a great word-of-mouth recommendation.

After a few weeks, the bow may start to get a little dirty. A bit tattered. Which is useful. Because it reminds the customer that they need to make a booking.

If you want to get more adventurous, try bandanas. These come ready-made in all kinds of colours. Or holiday themes. And are still relatively inexpensive. You may even consider getting some made with your logo or branding on them. So the dogs become little walking advertisements for your business.

Personally, I like bandanas. They may work for you with the right dog and customer. A grooming bow is small. Inoffensive. Cute. It doesn't interfere with the dog's overall look. Whereas a bandana, by comparison, is sometimes too much. But it doesn't hurt to try bandanas. Some customers will be thrilled.

Also, consider creative colouring. You get a ready-made stencil. Like a spooky ghost for Hallowe'en for example (FUN, right?). Maybe some Holly and berries at Christmas. Or a heart-shape at Valentines.

Simply place the stencil on a part of the dog. Perhaps along the top of the rear legs. Using pet-friendly colouring, spray over the top of the stencil. You've then created the pattern on the dog.

Creative colouring can be a real head-turner. It will guarantee lots of comments. And people will simply squeal with delight and say "isn't that just adorable?"

It's nice to have these occasional departures of hilarity from everyday seriousness. So, give it a whirl. Find a course on Creative Colouring. And try it out in your salon.

I love walking through the parks afterwards. The owners – and their dogs – will recognise me. I'll see the dogs with their little bows. Or bandanas. Or little pattern on their coat. "I did that," I'll say. To myself. And my heart will thump with pride. Sigh.

64. Holiday Bookings

If you've ever worked Christmas, you'll know that things can get pretty hectic. Not just Christmas. But certain other times of the year as well. Like just before the schools let out. And everybody takes off for their holidays.

So there will be a mad scramble for people to get their dogs groomed. Those with better time management skills will have made sure to book early. But we have many lovely regular clients who sometimes forget. We don't want to let down a regular client.

Despite our best efforts at telling clients to make sure they book well in advance for Christmas, some of them will plain forget. They'll even call you on the day - perhaps the Saturday before Christmas - and plead with you for a spot. By then, you've already probably got a waiting list.

So, you're not able to fit them in because they haven't planned well enough in advance. And it may be that your regular customer has to go elsewhere. Of course, this works the other way around too. You'll end up with new customers who left it too late with their regular groomer. They're now coming to you for their dog's Christmas grooming.

You can handle this a couple of ways. You could be dismissive and say, too bad, so sad, it's their fault. They should have booked sooner. This is true.

On the other hand, we're all busy. So it's kind of forgivable to forget. And I'd say try to squeeze the dog in somewhere. Maybe you can't do it on that day. Maybe you'll have to work later.

The customer will know it's their fault for leaving it too late. But if you go the extra mile to fit them in, they will appreciate it. And hopefully that appreciation will be demonstrated by a nice Christmas tip.

Now that they've booked, make sure they get a grooming appointment card with the date and time clearly written. Follow up with a phone call or text message reminder a day or two before the appointment.

Another issue is when our lovely client cancels their appointment. This is hugely aggravating. You will have already turned down two or more other clients for that coveted spot.

It's even more annoying when they simply don't show up. No phone call. No apology. And perhaps you even went out of your way to fit them in. It happens. This is life. And there is usually a simple and reasonable explanation for it. Don't allow yourself to get wound up about this sort of thing.

It's still lost revenue however. There are ways of addressing this for the busy periods like Christmas. If your appointments book is so full, and you basically have people competing for spaces to get their dog groomed, you can ask all customers to pre-pay. Inform them that if they miss their appointment, the fee is non-refundable. Nor can the fee be transferred to a booking at another time.

This way if the customer is a no-show, your business doesn't have to suffer because of somebody else's bad time-keeping. Reasonable people will understand this. They appreciate that you have a business to run. And if you are asking for pre-pay just in the holiday season, they won't be offended. Instead, they'll understand that you are a professional. That you run a tight ship.

And if they don't understand, then they're not being very sympathetic to you are they? And do you really want that kind of customer? Bend over backwards for your good customers. Not your bad ones.

65. Customer Waiting & Watching

PRECIOUS: Generally, your customers will be happy to leave their dog with you. You've told them how long you expect the grooming to take. And then they're off. To do really important things. Like shopping.

Occasionally though, you'll get the customer who wants to stay. And watch.

This can be frustrating. The owner's presence might be distracting for the dog. Or if they see their dog struggling on the table they'll even come into the salon. To help out. And this just makes matters worse.

In some cases, we ask the owner to stay. If the dog is old, for example. Or the dog is aggressive.

If the owner asks, don't make them feel unwelcome. You might prefer them elsewhere. But offer them a cup of coffee. Or point them to the coffee maker if you're busy.

And then establish your ground rules. Explain that you have to get on with the grooming without their interruption. Ask them to keep a distance. And avoid being seen by their dog while it's on the table. Or in the bath.

I need the dog to co-operate. I establish a dynamic between me and the dog. That gets undermined if the owner is clucking and coo-ing from the side-lines. It confuses the dog. And makes my grooming more difficult. More time consuming.

Some owners will think they can come right into the salon. Like a mum or dad holding their child's hand in the dentist's chair.

I have a sign on the door to my salon. No Unauthorised Persons Beyond This Point.

It's there so people don't open the door and let a dog escape. I can't take the risk of anything happening to the customer either. Like slipping on the floor. Because I'm not sure the insurance company would like this sort of thing.

A lot of salons are designed with the grooming 'in-view'. Which is great. It puts the customer's mind at ease. They can see that their dog is safe and happy. That their dog isn't being mishandled by a groomer having a bad day. So I'm happy for a customer to stay and watch.

I don't actively encourage it though. Some salons will have chairs for the customers in Reception. I don't. Because I don't have time to chat about the weather. Or catch up on the park gossip.

66. Tutoring Customers to Brush Their Dog's Coat

Often I have to take a dog short because the coat is matted. The customer is disappointed. I can see it in their face. Or they just plain tell me. With the occasional swear word thrown in.

So we'll check the records to see when they last came. In some cases, it could be months.

This is WAY too long for coats that require regular grooming.

If they want to keep length on the dog's coat, they have to come in more often. They might worry about the price. But if they commit to a regular schedule of every four to six weeks I can offer them a better deal. Maybe a free grooming with every sixth visit. Or a general 20 per cent off.

But taking the dog to the groomer is only one part of it. The customer needs to take some responsibility. They need to brush their dog at home. At least every couple of days.

It's good for bonding with the dog. It keeps the customer aware of their dog's health. With regular brushing, the customer will come across anything that doesn't look right. A tick. A mole. Skin irritation. Cuts or bumps.

So I tell them to brush their dog. If they don't want to brush, they need to see me more often!

The thing is, they might be brushing. They're just not doing it effectively. Maybe they're not even using the right brush.

In the section about matted dogs, I show Madame Marvellous how to brush her Yorkie, Fifi. I show her which brush to use. Fifi has a silky coat. And she's a small dog. So I use a small, soft pin, slicker.

I provide a demonstration. But I show her the fiddly bits too. She likes Fifi to have a long skirt. A long tail. To have length on the head. So that she can attach a little bow.

I do this with plenty of customers. I'll tell them to follow me into the styling section of the salon. I put their dog on the table. Take them through the motions. Exactly as I've done with Fifi. Make them try it. I'll confirm they own the right brush for the dog's coat. If not, I'll sell them one from the shop.

Customers love this kind of individual attention. It feels like special treatment. Especially if you have a sign on your door that says 'Authorized Persons Only.' And they get to come through. To the other side. The bright side.

So I actively encourage you to do it with your customers. The benefits are worth it. A better educated customer. Somebody who is more engaged with their responsibility to brush their dog regularly. A dog that will benefit from better maintenance of its coat.

67. Not My Fault

What happens when a cut is NOT the groomer's fault? Dogs are prone to getting various cuts and nicks. These can be so minor that the owner hasn't even noticed. The cut has simply healed naturally. And a scab has formed.

Guess what happens when the dog is put into the tub. And shampooed vigorously in warm water.

No points for getting this one right. The scab comes loose. And depending on how old the cut is, it could bleed. Suddenly the water draining from tub is tinged with pink. And we freak out.

This will be totally confusing. We haven't gotten anywhere close to touching the dog with a pair of scissors. And suddenly the dog is bleeding.

In this situation we need to take a closer look at the cut and administer first-aid. Hold a sterilised cloth or towel against the wound. Apply pressure to stop any bleeding. Inspect the wound.

With an old wound that has re-opened, the bleeding will be slight. In most cases, you should be able to complete grooming the dog. But first, you need to inform the customer.

This is where it gets tricky. My policy with my own grooming – and this is something I tell all my students – is simply to tell the truth. Be 100 per cent upfront about what has happened.

Most customers, in my experience, will accept your explanation. It can happen that the customer suspects you of having cut their dog. They suspect that you are making it up about a scab coming loose in the bath.

This reminds us of the importance of a full health-check and thorough inspection of the coat and skin during the pre-grooming consultation. Because it helps to avoid exactly this type of situation.

68. Vet Said The Groomer Did It

Now let's look at another cause of misery for us down-trodden dog groomers.

Let's imagine a scenario. The dog and its owner have happily left your salon after a successful grooming. Then, a couple of days later, you get a phone call. The owner is unhappy because they've just come from the vet. The dog has some kind of skin rash. And it's your fault.

In fact, it could very well be that you noticed the dog had bit of a skin problem. Maybe you even re-assured the customer that it's nothing serious. However, they should consider a better diet for their dog. Perhaps even a cod liver oil supplement.

So here is what's happened. After grooming the owner has evidently noticed the skin problem. Might just have been clipper irritation. They've taken their dog to the vet. The vet asks all kinds of questions. The owner tells the vet that their dog has recently been groomed.

Not to take anything away from the vet, but that makes for a very simple diagnosis.

"The grooming caused it."

Maybe the dog has had some kind of reaction to the shampoo you are using in your salon.

Maybe the dog was badly matted before grooming. The removal of knots and tangles have caused some skin irritation. Or even revealed a pre-existing skin irritation.

The vet isn't out to pass the buck onto the groomer. The vet simply may have explained to the owner that the skin irritation is BECAUSE of the grooming. The vet will provide some treatment or anti-biotic to reduce the inflammation.

Yes, the grooming may have brought about the irritation or inflammation. But it's not the groomer's fault.

When a customer says that my grooming has caused a problem with their dog, they'll expect me to refund them. In full. And to pick up the vet bill.

Here is what I do. I consult my own records. I review the information there. I might well have written that the dog was badly matted. If the dog developed clipper irritation or its skin is inflamed, it's likely this was because of the matting. Of having to shave the skin to get rid of the mats.

By shaving the dog I am in fact 'treating' the dog to prevent worse things happening. I explain this all to the customer. Often they'll understand. But if they still insist that my grooming has caused injury and 'the vet says so' I'll speak to the vet.

I call the vet and have a conversation with him or her directly. Frankly, I don't like being accused of something that isn't my fault. Certainly not when the grooming I have provided is, in fact, beneficial for the dog.

In the conversation with the vet I usually discover that the customer's claims have been ever so slightly skewed. Funny that.

I discover that the vet explained that, yes, the grooming may have caused the skin irritation. But the vet was unaware the dog was badly matted.

In other situations, it might be impossible to prove that the grooming caused an injury. The vet is only putting two and two together. It's a coincidence that the dog went for grooming. And now there's a problem.

I will ask the vet to put in writing his or her claim that the grooming caused the problem. The vet is unlikely to do this unless it's a clear case - for example, perhaps a scissor cut that went completely undetected during the grooming. It does happen.

So, I have to make a business decision. If I have explained everything to the customer. Including my conversation with the vet. And that the vet is unwilling to put in writing that the grooming caused the dog a problem, I won't refund the customer. Nor pick up the vet bill.

On the other hand, when all parties generally agree that the dog has an injury which could only have been caused by grooming - and for some reason this went undetected in the salon - then yes I will pick up the vet bill. I will apologise. And I'll offer a 50 per cent discount off the customer's next grooming.

It's up to you but in a lot of salons in the US, more so than in the UK, customers are asked to sign a legal waiver. This is to reduce the salon's financial liability if an accident happens that is outside of their control.

Dogs are unpredictable. Accidents will happen. It comes down ultimately to keeping the dog healthy and the customer happy. But don't allow yourself to be taken advantage of either if you are not in the wrong.

69. Customer Complaint

You can't please all of the people all of the time. You will groom a dog. You'll do a good job. You'll be proud.

The customer will show up. They'll see their dog. They might say thank you. Pay. And leave. And you'll never hear from them again.

Suddenly you'll end up with a critical review online.

But the customer might also break into a hysterical fit. In your salon. In front of other customers.

I once witnessed a lady start sobbing so violently she had to sit down on the floor. She cradled her little dog in her lap. Rocked her back and forth. Her shoulders convulsed. A loud torturous wail filled the shop.

She wasn't just disappointed. She was devastated.

I remember feeling sorry for the dog.

Thankfully, I've only seen seriously distressed customers a few times. But I have had my share of complaints.

Usually the complaint is that I've taken the dog too short. The customer wanted to keep the coat long. They wanted to keep the furnishings. What have I done to the tail?

In most cases, I had to go short because the customer hadn't maintained the coat. There were knots or matting that I couldn't (or wouldn't) brush out. So it had to go short.

But why are they complaining if they knew what to expect?

This is the reason we do the pre-grooming consultation. To manage customer expectations.

During the consultation we establish what we can achieve with the dog's coat. I will discuss this with the customer. I'll make sure they understand. I don't want any surprises when they collect their dog.

So a complaint isn't about my grooming. It's about me failing to manage the customer expectations. But, sure, I can still get a complaint about my grooming. I'll listen patiently to what the customer has to say. I need to understand what they're unhappy about. So I can respond to it.

They might be angry and upset. The words they use might be really colourful. Or it might be entirely reasonable.

For example, they may point out that the cut is uneven. That it's not balanced. That the length on one ear is different from the other. The length on the body doesn't blend into the legs.

I will look at the dog with them to see what they're talking about. I won't be defensive. I'll just try to keep an open mind.

They could be right. I might have missed something. So I'll offer to correct it for them.

It might be a day or two before they've noticed. That's fine. Usually all it takes is a quick bit of scissoring.

The correction will be made. The dog will look better. The customer will feel better. No hard feelings.

All sounds wonderful. In fact, those complaints warm my heart a little. Because it means that the dog owner cares.

I can handle those. It's more like feedback. It becomes a collaborative effort between me and the customer to come to the right solution. To make it 'just so'.

I would rather a customer say something than nothing. That way, we can resolve it. The alternative is that I just never hear from them again. They've had a negative experience. And it's now out of my control.

There is an expression. Make a customer happy and they'll tell TWO friends. Make a customer unhappy, and they'll tell TEN friends.

So I prefer to make customers happy. I prefer the feedback. So I can resolve it there and then.

70. I Am Running Late with My Grooming

PRECIOUS: Colin is a good time-keeper. And he is good at managing customer expectations. During the pre-grooming consultation, he will tell the customer when their dog will be ready.

Sometimes though, something happens in the salon. Maybe we took too long brushing out another dog. Or another customer showed up late. And now we're running behind.

That two hours we promised the customer? It's going to be three. Maybe more.

It's really important to let your customer know that you're running late. Otherwise they show up expecting to collect their dog. And you have to tell them "Oh, sorry, it's going to be another hour."

Make sure therefore you've got their telephone number when they leave. Ideally their mobile number. If you're running behind, send them a simple text message apologising. You'll need an extra 30 minutes.

The buzzword for this is 'communicate'.

Most customers won't mind. A few might be put out. But as long as you've let them know in good time, it won't be a problem. But if they've made a wasted journey because you didn't let them know, then they have a right to be upset.

71. Late Customer / No-Show

I arrive early at work. At least a good hour before the doors open. I like to ease into the day. I grab the appointments book. A strong cup of coffee. Milk and two sugars, please. And a muffin. I'll double-check to make sure everybody has been sent a reminder text message. Email. Or telephone call. So there shouldn't be any surprises about anybody forgetting their appointment.

I work out in my mind how the day will look. I'll recognise the regulars. Like Archie the Miniature Schnauzer. He's a bit fidgety on the table. So he'll take a little bit longer. Oh, and there's Betty the Newfoundland. For a bath and brush. She's a big dog. Good, she's been booked for three hours. I've got one of my students on her.

Everything looks under control. Should be a good day. By the time I've had my second muffin, we're ready to open.

The phone rings. Archie is running late. Stuck in traffic. The owner is really sorry. She'll be here as soon as possible.

My little plan for the day needs adjusting. I'm not upset. I just need to re-think things.

Archie is going to be 30 minutes late. If I get somebody else to come in early, it'll be 30 minutes before they get here. Then I have the conflict of both dogs at the same time. So I leave it. I'll just try to make it up during the day. I may take less time for lunch.

If Archie's owner said she would still be an hour, then I'd have somebody else come in early. We'll get to Archie afterwards.

Seems a reasonable solution. The owner will understand.

About half of my customers are good at letting me know if they'll be late. The other ones don't say anything. If there is no sign of them for fifteen minutes, I'll call them. Usually they're just in the middle of parking. Or they're just down the road. They'll be right with me.

Sometimes, despite reminding them the day before, they've completely forgotten. So they may have to re-schedule.

As you'd expect, I get frustrated when I hear nothing from the customer. Fifteen minutes and I can't get hold of them. Twenty minutes. Still nothing. Thirty minutes. Nada.

That's my cut-off point. I'll call somebody to ask them to come in early. Usually, they can. Often I'll have a list of customers who want to come in if there is a cancellation. So I can try one of them.

If, in the meantime, the late customer shows up, I'll see what we can do. If there is still time, I'll take them in. They are a paying customer, after all. If they are sincerely apologetic, I'll just ask them, please, make sure to let us know next time.

I get frustrated by the oblivious customers. They have no idea they are late. Or they don't think it matters. Except when they have to wait for you of course.

Life is like that. If you run a restaurant. A bowling alley. If you're a dentist. Some customers are just late. For everything. For life.

It screws up my day. My carefully made plan is ruined. I don't like it when that happens.

I will always try to fit the customer in however. If I can't, then I'll have to re-book. But when I re-book, I ask for the full grooming fee up-front. I think this is reasonable. If they object, then they are welcome to be late somewhere else.

I don't like to lose business of course. But I won't be walked over either.

It's not simple black and white of course. You have to apply common sense. For a first-time offender or a new customer, I will explain my policy. Maybe I'll just ask for a 50 per cent deposit. Or warn them. If it happens again, I'll have to ask for the full fee up-front.

It's the repeat offending I want to avoid. With repeat offenders I will insist on the full fee. It's funny how they always arrive on time after I do that.

Then we have the so-called 'No Shows'.

I do my best to remind people a day or two before their appointment. It works really well. But sometimes I still get the occasional no-show. In a lot of cases, the excuse is perfectly legitimate. The dog is ill. Had to go the vet. A family member has died (not to be insensitive, but I hear this one a lot). The car got stuck in the snow.

Like the late customer, I'll re-book. But I'll insist on the full fee up-front. That way I don't have to be the one who loses out.

I also add the No Shows to my 'Blacklist'. A friend of mine calls it her 'ShihTzulist'. Not necessarily to do with Shih-Tzus. More about that in the next section.

72. Blacklist & Whitelist

My Blacklist is my record of customers that I have fired. Either I refuse to book them. Or I demand a full or partial payment up-front.

The customers I refuse are people who are more trouble than it's worth.

See the frying pan incident that Precious describes in 'The Customer is Always Right.' The frying pan guy is a perfect candidate for my Blacklist.

Or it could be a dog that, for love or money, I just can't groom. I'm not being nasty about this. Maybe I just can't control the dog on the table. Despite my best efforts. You have to know when to say No.

Others on the Blacklist would include the repeat-offending No Shows. The ones who refuse to pay upfront.

Or it could be somebody who is just plain unreasonable. Like the customer I can never please. The one who will always find something wrong. And expect a discount.

I've also added the occasional person I've never met. That's because I've been warned about them by another salon. For example, the woman who tried to pay with funny money. Or the guy who refuses to pay because he's disappointed. But he's tried this on at several salons.

These things happen rarely. But they can happen. If it happens to me, I'll call round the other salons. And warn them.

So that's my Blacklist.

What about my Whitelist?

My Whitelist is the record of customers I love. Sure, I love all my customers. But there are a few I can count on for a number of things.

We get requests all the time from the media. They're looking to write a 'feel good' story about something dog-related. Customers on my Whitelist are the ones I'll contact.

Madame Marvellous and her Yorkie, Fifi, are on my Whitelist. That's because Madame M imagines that Fifi is destined for greatness. She's desperate for a profile in a magazine or newspaper. With anybody. Anywhere.

Other customers could include dogs that are really good specimens for competing. I often have former students ask me if I can recommend a dog. I'll refer to my Whitelist.

Sometimes, I'll also have a gap in my bookings. Or I'll need a specific breed of dog for one of my students. For example, I'll need a Border so that I can train a student in hand-stripping. The customer is accommodating. And they're happy to get a discount for helping out. So they're on my Whitelist.

Don't be scared by the fact that I have to keep a Blacklist. There aren't many people on it. And I can happily report that my Whitelist is much bigger than my Blacklist.

73. The Customer is Always Right

PRECIOUS: I am a retail fiend. I could be a professional shopper. And one of the things I like most about my weekly retail therapy? Discovering GREAT customer service.

Having spent a lot of years in the States, I was always impressed by the whole 'service with a smile' ethos. I don't need the waiter to be my best friend for the evening. But I appreciated the personal touch. The eagerness to please.

Although things are changing in the UK, customer service is still poor by comparison. It's a cultural difference. American style chumminess in the sock department wouldn't really work here. But there is stuff that UK retailers and service providers can learn.

For example, a famous American retailer came up with the expression "The customer is always right." He wanted all the employees in his department store to accept this. Not because he believed it to be true. But because an unhappy customer is a powerful negative force. And that can hurt your business.

It's a marketing strategy.

A customer comes into a retail shop. They buy an article of clothing. Or some homeware. Maybe a lava lamp. A week later, they return the item. It's faulty. Or there's a defect. They'd like a full refund.

It's easier to keep the customer happy. Even if the item can't be re-sold and the business loses ten bucks, or a hundred. It's not worth getting into an argument with the customer. Because then you'll upset the customer.

Which reminds me of a friend's story about a customer returning a frying pan. The customer had clearly been using the frying pan. For about a year. He liked his fry-ups. The pan was blackened from use. And it was still greasy. He hadn't even bothered to clean it. And now the handle was a little loose. It only needed a screw tightening. But he wanted to return it. For a full refund. He was being stubborn. And vocal.

I would have grabbed that frying pan and knocked him over the head.

My friend, though, is a little more even-tempered than me. She provided the refund. Then added the customer's details to the shop's Blacklist. In case he tried this sort of thing again in another department.

Dog grooming, of course, is different from retail. We are providing a service. We have a skill. A craft. It requires training. And experience.

That makes us experts. The customer might be making grumbling noises because they're disappointed by the haircut. You could be convinced that this is the breed standard. This is how it should be.

I'm tempted to re-write the expression: "The Groomer is Always Right."

But I won't.

Let's say the customer is making a big deal of it. Taking up my time. Making a scene in the salon. Generally, I cut my losses. I try to avoid a long drawn-out affair of he-said, she-said blah blah.

I tell them I'm so sorry they're disappointed. I offer them a 20 per cent discount on the next grooming. When would they like to come in?

Provided this isn't a customer who tries it on all the time, I may even offer a 50 per cent discount.

If it is somebody who whines constantly, then this is a customer I can do without.

I will fire the customer.

Which means I will put them on my Blacklist.

If I have a history of that customer constantly moaning and getting discounts out of me, it's not worth it any longer. So I apologise profusely. I explain that, unfortunately, we're not able to meet their expectations. And I'm afraid they will have to go elsewhere from now on.

Yes, I risk their wrath. I risk a bad online review.

For the most part, my online reviews are good. The occasional bad review isn't such a bad thing. It gives legitimacy to the good reviews. Any sensible customer can appreciate this. And it's the sensible customers I want to attract. Not the guy with the frying pan.

74. Tips / Gratuities

PRECIOUS: I love going out and about. To restaurants. Clubs. The bowling lanes. Taking taxis. Visiting the hairdressers. Getting my nails done.

Other nights I like to stay at home. Order a pizza. Or Chinese food.

And everywhere I turn, I'm tipping. The waiter. The cabbie. The stylist. The manicurist. The delivery guy.

In fact, sometimes I have no choice. A 'discretionary' service charge has been added. The tip is built into the bill. But then I even leave a tip on top of that. Sheesh.

So what about dog groomers?

Should we expect tips?

It's fair to compare our jobs to that of human stylists. They get tips. From me anyway.

Of course, it depends where you live. There might be a cultural expectation of tipping. Or you might live and work somewhere that it's unusual. I've lived in the US for many years. And in the UK. There is a difference.

Receiving a tip is nice. Not just because a few dollars will help to pay for a Starbucks latte. But it's recognition for a good job. That makes us feel good about ourselves. And the dog. And the dog's owner.

Generally, I think a bit of customer education can help. Dog grooming is a tip-able service. People might not know that. They might not agree.

There are ways of 'encouraging' their awareness.

I won't recommend hanging up the sign that says 'Tipping is not a city in China'. Not subtle enough. A little bit tacky. But it is very funny.

Instead, I would suggest placing a smart vase on your counter. With a nicely presented sign. Something that says "Please help me further my grooming education". Add a flyer next to the vase promoting a course you want to do. For example, that Creative Colouring workshop you want to attend. Or the Professional Refresher Course at the Colin Taylor Academy (to use a random example).

Your customer won't take offence. It's a nice little prompt to leave something in the pot. Their change. Or a couple of extra pounds or dollars. They'll probably feel good about it. Knowing they are contributing to a worthwhile cause.

What's more, they'll appreciate that you want to improve your skills. Especially after the last job you did on their dog. I'm teasing.

Be honest about it. That is, make sure you actually go to the course.

You'll want to report back to any interested customers. They have contributed to your further education. So they may ask you how it went.

You might feel uneasy taking this approach. You can always just plonk a tasteful little tip jar near the cash-till. Attach a cute little 'Thank You' card. With a smiley-face.

III. The Grooming Salon

75. Design & Layout

PRECIOUS: I love style and design. I like things to look wonderfully sparkly and clean. I love salons that smell wonderful. Make sure to read my section on 'smelly shop'. And I love a salon that is laid out well.

With salon design, the most important considerations are safety and practicality. This has priority over the aesthetics.

There are three main parts to a salon. Ideally, try to keep them separate. It depends, of course, on the size of your premises.

1. Reception. This is where your customers come to deliver their dogs. If you have retail, this is where you will have your products on display. You will keep your appointments book here. And the till.

It's also the first impression of your salon. You never get a second chance to make a first impression. So keep it clean. Bright. Organised. Wonderful.

2. Styling area. This is the dedicated area for your tables. Where you style and scissor your dogs. Must be clean and bright with good lighting. So think about light-coloured walls. Plenty of mirrors.

Make sure it's free of clutter. If you have the space, try to keep this area separate from your wet room area. You want it to be less 'industrial'. Separate from the noise of the blaster and dryer.

Design a space that allows you to relax. So that you can concentrate on your styling. Your scissoring. Or be a bit creative. You can even play soft music in here. To soothe your dog's nerves. Or your own.

3. Wet room area. This is your area for bathing and drying. Make sure you have non-slip floors. Try to locate it to the rear of your salon. Not only is it wet, it's noisy. The sound of blasters and dryers.

It's the 'industrial' area of your shop. Very important to keep clear of any clutter. Or cables trailing along the floor.

Absolute must: keep the reception separate from your grooming salon with two sets of doors or gates. We call it an 'air-lock space'. This is critical. You never want to have just one door through which the dog can escape into the front.

With respect to equipment like your table, bath or dryers, this of course depends on your budget. You need the basics to get going. So, if you are limited by your budget, just make sure to get the basic equipment first. So that you can actually start grooming. Once your business develops, you can re-invest part of your earnings into better quality products.

76. Tools & Equipment

Many of my students go on to open their own salons. They'll often ask my advice about tools and equipment. What bath do I recommend? What table? What shears? Clippers?

They will do their research. Pick up catalogues from various suppliers. Ooh and aah at the sophisticated new products. But what attracts the eye might not be the most practical. A grooming salon is industrial. So I go with the tried and tested. Something solid and durable. Not too many bells and whistles. Not too many moving parts. And I try to minimise the potential for electric cables. Invariably, they get in the way. Or blow a fuse.

I look for a good local supplier. So that I can get them on the phone, in my time-zone. And I choose a brand that can supply replacement parts quickly if anything breaks.

Bath – I like a big metal tub. Perhaps with a sliding door on it for ease of access. It should also have a hydraulic lift. So that it moves up or down. This makes it easier to get a large, heavy dog in the tub. Or adjust the height so that it's at the right level for the person bathing. The lift doesn't have to be electric. That means another cable I have to tuck away so nobody trips over it.

Table – I like a table with a large platform. The heavier the better. Must also have a hydraulic lift. Electric or manual is fine. I like a strong, sturdy frame. I don't need the table to come with anything additional. Like lighting under the platform. Or specially designed holders for my scissors. Just a shelf underneath is fine.

Stand Dryer – there are a lot of dryers on the market. Generally, the more expensive they are, the better they are. But you can find a good workhorse at a reasonable price. I prefer the ones that I can attach to the wall or ceiling. It might limit being able to roll them across the floor. To the other end of the salon. But I love the fact that they don't take up floor space. With yet more electric cables just waiting to snake around your ankles. I avoid the portable dryers that you can tuck under your arm. It's not a natural fit for the way I work.

Blaster – A good blaster can really cut down your drying time. Invest in a good blaster. Make sure it includes a hot air setting and variable speed.

Those are the main pieces of equipment you'll need. Then, of course, you have your tools. Scissors. Clippers. Brushes. Combs. Security straps. I cover some of these separately. The critical thing is to treat your tools with respect.

77. Choosing Clippers

Clippers are essential. But make sure you choose the right clippers for you. These have to feel comfortable in your hand and you should be able to manoeuvre across the dog's body easily.

The technology improvements in recent years means you can now choose cordless clippers as well. You can appreciate that this is much easier, and SAFER, than having to manage a cord while you are clipping.

Rule of thumb with respect to clippers: you must make absolutely sure you have a spare set in case one of them conks out on you. Not a good thing to happen. Especially on a busy Saturday or in the Christmas period.

Clippers are machines with little motors that require regular servicing. Just like your car, if you don't get it serviced occasionally, it's going to break down. I suggest you send your clippers to get serviced every six months. This depends of course on how busy you are. But if you are using your clippers on five or six dogs a day, five or six days a week then yes, get them serviced AT LEAST every six months. If you are not as busy as that, then maybe every nine months. Just don't leave it too late.

Yep, it's true. Clippers don't come cheap and getting them serviced regularly also adds up. But they are extremely good value when you consider how much revenue they earn for you. So don't skimp on a good set of clippers. Make the additional investment to ensure you've got the best and strongest clippers. The extra money now will save you all kinds of headaches later.

If you've made the transition to cordless clippers, always make sure to have your base charger plugged in. Let your battery go completely flat before replacing with the second battery.

As for brands, I think it's best if you make sure to buy the same brand blade to match the brand of clipper. Yes, they'll say all blades are universal but I don't agree. I know from my own experience that different brand blades sometimes just don't sit quite right on different model clippers.

If by chance you have two clippers and let's say a 7F blade works on one clipper but not on the other, the problem is with the clipper, not the blade. Your clipper needs servicing.

78. Choosing Scissors

PRECIOUS: I admit it. I'm a sucker for good scissors. I know I'm not alone. Male or female. Young or not-so-young. Gay or straight. Scissors are like shoes. We just can't resist a wonderful pair. The shapes. The curves. The colours. My fingers twitch with excitement when I come across a new set. I start to see them in my dreams. Creating beautiful shapes.

Yes, like shoes, scissors come in an array of sizes. Colours. Makes. Models. But, like shoes, they also need to fit. However much you might need that particular pair, right now, if they don't feel right, don't try to convince yourself you have to have them.

The colour of the scissors won't improve your scissor work. And after a few days, the euphoria of our purchase will reside. We might still love them. But, fundamentally, scissors have to be comfortable. They have to be practical. We need to be able to use them with ease. They are the extension of our hands. The instruments of our talent. Our training. Our expertise. So don't be swayed by the salesman's perfect pitch. Go with the feelings in your hands. But also your gut.

Let's say you have acquired that prized pair of scissors. You have to keep them in good working order. You have to make sure you use them only in ways that will protect their balance and sharpness. It's hardly any wonder that heated arguments break out when a pair of scissors is borrowed without permission. And fights over scissors – sharp tools, remember – can be a frightening thing.

You'll need to use different scissors for different parts of grooming. Use a small, cheaper scissor around the feet. Because if you hit a dog's nail with your prized scissors, this can damage the blades, even to a tiny degree. Use a wider bladed shear for scissoring dirty hair. These blades can take the wear and tear of cutting heavy dirty coats. And then go for a lighter or Japanese style shear as your finishing scissors. The technology of scissors, the materials used in the construction, is complex and scientific. Look out for the 'Rockwell' hardness of the metal used. A harder Rockwell hardness means stronger metals have been used. Which is what you'll want.

When I buy a pair of scissors, this is what I do: I always feel them in my hands first. To check for a good, natural fit. I check the Rockwell hardness. I want something that is going to be strong and durable. I don't get distracted by how glamorous or pretty they look. I concentrate on the potential performance. But it takes enormous self-discipline.

I try to go for an off-set shear when buying a pair of scissors. This means that the thumb hole is higher than the finger hole. My collection of scissors include:

Curves – to get nice angles and lines.
Straight shears – all purpose.
Thinning shears – to blend in lines.
Texturising shears (chunkers)- create a more jagged / textured look.

Scissors also have tension screws. Adjust this so it feels right. But resist fiddling with it too much. When I store my scissors, I make sure they don't bang against each other. I also don't store them in the wet room area of the salon. There is a lot of condensation here. I need to put them in a cool, dry place.

I have so much experience buying and using scissors, I should create my own pair. I'll call them 'Precious'.

79. Shampoos & Treatments

PRECIOUS: I am fanatical about shampoos! I love trying new ones out. So I'll look through the catalogues. Contact the suppliers. Ask for free samples.

Then I'll find something I absolutely love. I'm not just talking about the label. I can see through the marketing.

I have to test it out. I have to feel the volume when I'm bathing a dog. I have to feel the difference in my scissoring. The right shampoo will have that difference. It will be something special.

Of course, I pay attention to the price. Need to operate profitably after all. Sure, I can buy at the top end. But the dilution rate and the price per gallon might make it too expensive.

So I usually stick with my mid-range shampoos. I always find something I'm really happy with. At minimum, the shampoo needs to replenish the coat. Keep its natural texture and oils. Be gentle on the skin.

Some salons will offer a range of treatments. Ultra-mild hypoallergenic. Oatmeal and Honey. Aloe Vera. Jojoba. Pumpkin and sunflowers. Vanilla mist. It all sounds so delicious. I will sell bottles of these types of shampoos in the shop. But in the salon, I keep it simple. I have a general purpose shampoo. A Whitener. A Puppy. A flea. And maybe a volumising shampoo.

I also pay attention to the dilution rates. Ideally, I'd like to get a 15 to 1 ratio. That is, from one gallon, I will get 15 gallons to wash with.

Often you'll notice dogs with dry, flaky skin. It could be related to diet. But it might also mean that the dog is being shampooed too often. With the wrong type of shampoo.

A dog's coat and skin has lots of natural oils. Shampooing frequently will strip the coat of its natural oils. But it depends on the shampoo. Supermarket varieties can be too harsh. Whereas many new shampoos with all-natural ingredients are safe to use once a week. The shampoos I use in our salon can be used weekly. No problem.

You might get asked by a customer if they can use human shampoo on their dog. The short answer (because this all gets very complex), is No. Human shampoo is pH balanced for specific application to human skin and hair. Same applies for dogs. And these pH balances are different.

This is not to say it would be a problem. Years ago, my mother would occasionally use a famous brand of baby shampoo on our dog. I don't think there was any adverse reaction. But I'd resist getting into this conversation with your customers.

I have yet to see a shampoo that is marketed for both human and canine use. Until that happens, I'd tell the customer to continue using their own shampoo on their own hair. And the dog's shampoo on the dog's hair.

80. Health & Safety

Yesterday I hung up the Health and Safety poster in my salon. I accidentally pricked my finger on the thumb tack. My finger started to bleed insanely. Like a little spouting fountain of red blood. I needed a band-aid urgently.

But where's the first-aid kit? I started looking frantically through the cardboard recycling. But no luck. Finally, there it was. Under a pile of fresh-laundered towels.

I managed to leave a blood-trail across all those boxes and towels. I'm lucky not to have bled to death in the time it took me to find the first-aid kit. I can imagine the police investigator. Finding my lifeless corpse in the salon. Re-tracing my dying steps.

"And here," says the Inspector, standing next to the crooked Health and Safety poster, "he received the fatal prick on his index finger. From the blood splatter analysis, we see he rummaged through this stack of cardboard boxes. And came to his unfortunate demise. Collapsed in a pile of fresh laundry. It was a soft landing. With a pleasant fragrance of lavender."

Alright, so pricking my finger with a thumb tack isn't the greatest medical emergency known to humankind. But it made me realise the importance of a dedicated first-aid station. Clearly marked. Easily accessible.

Yes, I am talking about a HUMAN First Aid kit. But what about a PET first aid kit? Can we apply human first aid treatment to dogs?

The short answer is this: never, ever use any kind of human-grade medication on a dog or cat. That includes aspirin or any disinfectant that you would normally use on yourself. You can use alcohol-free iodine and antibiotic creams on dog cuts. But double-check that the treatment you are getting is suitable for animals.

But first aid for a cat or dog is less about administering medication. That's the vet's job. It's a secondary action to take after a dog has been injured.

The 'first' in first-aid is what you do first with a cat or dog that has been injured in your salon. If this is a cut, make sure you cover it with a clean wet towel. Apply pressure to help stop the bleeding. Get the cat or dog to the vet.

You will also need to have Fire Exit signs. And fire extinguishers. Visibly marked with little red signs.

Your grooming salon isn't a kitchen. Or a Chemistry lab. Or a paint warehouse. So you'll normally just need to get a regular fire extinguisher. An ABC. To control Type A, B or C fires. This covers everyday material like paper or wood. Any flammable liquids like some cleaning products. As well as electrical (like faulty sockets or an appliance).

If a fire breaks out in your salon, and you think you can control or isolate it, use common sense. You've got a big bath with good pressure on it. So you can use water from the bath.

You will also need a prominent sign on the door to your salon. Something that says 'No Entry - Authorized Persons Only'. Your customers must know never to open your salon door. Arguably your biggest risk, every day, is a dog escaping.

Keep an Accident and Emergency log book. So that anytime there is an accident in your salon, it's recorded. It might be a groomer slipping on a wet floor and bumping her head. Or the accidental snip of a dog's ear. Write down the time and date. Describe the incident. Record the action taken.

This isn't simply about ticking the boxes on a form for the local council. Or the insurance companies. Even if you are a one-woman show, make sure your grooming salon follows 'best practise' when it comes to Health and Safety.

Which is what I was doing when I had my unfortunate accident. I thought it would be responsible of me to hang a Health and Safety poster in the salon. And it is. But I got a little too excited about things. That's how I pricked my finger. Anyway, all is better now. My finger has healed. The Health and Safety poster is hanging up straight.

81. Personal Protective Equipment

Since reading my Health and Safety poster, I've been paying more attention to the importance of the right kind of equipment we need to wear in the salon.

In the UK, when you study for your grooming qualifications, one of the modules is Health and Safety. It includes PPE. Personal Protective Equipment.

There are all kinds of hazards in the salon. For example (this is not an exhaustive list):

* wet and slippery floors
* noise from the blasters
* the air is filled with sharp tiny hairs flying about
* electrical cords on the floor
* poor lighting

So to minimise the risk of an accident or health complications, we wear Personal Protective Equipment.

Wear shoes that have a non-slip rubber sole. But they have to be comfortable because you're on your feet all day.

Wear ear plugs. You don't want to damage your hearing from prolonged exposure to the noise of blasters and dryers.

Wear goggles. Your eyes might get the occasional sharp little hair from the dogs you are grooming. Especially useful grooming double-coated breeds.

Wear a face mask. You don't want to inhale all the tiny dust particles and hair fragments that fill the air during grooming. This is a risk that we tend not to take very seriously. But overtime these small fibrous bits can get into our lungs. So you might have to look like a cyclist in Mexico City during grooming. But it will be safer for you in the long run.

Wear a hair-repellent tabard. This is your grooming uniform. It helps prevent the hair from getting into your skin. They can be like annoying little slivers of wood. Irritating and painful.

Like my section on Health and Safety in the salon, wearing PPE is not a guarantee of your health and safety. You have to exercise common sense. And personally, I struggle wearing a mask. I find it ridiculously uncomfortable. And hot. Instead, I make sure there is an open window and a good draft through the salon.

One thing I have changed is that I now wear ear plugs. I never used to. Because I was young and invincible. But now I struggle with my hearing. I don't want it to get any worse if I can help it.

You have to take personal responsibility on this one. If you work for a large corporate, it's likely they've told you all these things. You've had to put your signature against a declaration that you understand the risks.

If you fail to take personal responsibility and follow the recommended protective measures, then that's up to you. But you are putting your health at risk. My advice: be sensible. Wear the PPE. Adapt your grooming as necessary.

82. Blasters & Your Hearing

"WHAT? What did you say? No, I don't eat sportscars with my asparagus candles… what ARE you talking about?"

How much are you shouting in the salon over the roar of a blaster? And how much are you misunderstanding? Yep, the salon can be a noisy place. We like to advertise our salons as serene and calming. Peaceful and holistic. But the atmosphere can be more 'industrial'.

So what about this constant noise? Several years of this constant exposure can permanently damage your hearing. So are you taking the right precautions? Are you wearing earplugs?

A lot of friends of mine suffer from Tinnitus. Sure, it might have to do with cranking the volume on a Sony Walkman when they were younger. But it could also be about failing to wear ear plugs in a noisy salon.

You know when you've been to a loud concert? And afterwards your ears are ringing for a couple of hours? Well, imagine that the ringing doesn't stop. It stays with you constantly. The more annoyed you get by this ringing, the louder it gets. This is Tinnitus.

There is no reliable cure. Specialists generally advise sufferers to learn to live with it. We are, by nature, adaptable. So, depending on the severity of the ringing (it might also be a constant high pitch), you may learn eventually to ignore it.

Constant exposure to the blasters may also cause partial deafness. If you are the owner of a grooming salon, it is your responsibility to make sure your employees understand the Health and Safety requirements. This isn't just about first aid or cleaning up a wet floor. It also covers the other risks to our health - like hearing and the constant exposure to loud noise. Better safe than sorry. Because you really do want to protect your hearing.

83. Physical Demands of Grooming

PRECIOUS: Make no mistake. Grooming dogs is hard, physical work. You are constantly lifting the dogs. Onto the table. Into the bath. You're standing on your feet all day. Your forearms will ache from hour after hour of brushing. Your back is killing you. You've got dishpan hands from bathing that Newfoundland. You sweat. You ache. You need a long hot bath after a normal day.

Here is a quick checklist of things I do to make it easier on me.

I watch my posture. A friend of mine has been in and out of the doctor. She would always hunch over a dog she was grooming. She did this for years. She might have been standing. Or sitting on a high stool. But she would hunch. So now she's got a knotted up neck and shoulders. And has to go for sports massage weekly. Which is nice. But she's in a lot of pain.

I move around the table. Instead of standing in one place and moving the dog to suit me. It helps sometimes to have Kylie on the stereo.

I always lift with my knees. If a dog is too heavy, I ask a colleague for help. For the most part, I don't have to lift a heavy dog. Because...

Hydraulic table and bath. These go up and down. Either manual or electric. I don't try to be a hero. I use the hydraulic lift.

I wear the best shoes. They're comfortable. With orthopaedic soles. Okay, they're not glamorous. But another friend of mine - not the hunching one – developed terrible varicose veins. So I do what I can to protect my feet and legs. The floor in the salon, under the linoleum, is concrete. It's hard. Sometimes I'll stand on an orthopaedic mat so it's not as bad.

I stay hydrated. Lots of water during the day.

I pace myself. I take breaks. And days off. To recover. But also to preserve my sanity.

This is not a complete list. When I was younger, I was oblivious to the aches and pains. But after a few years of grooming, it can take its toll. Rather than wait for my body to break down, I do things to minimise the potential wear and tear.

84. Who Let The Dogs Out

Do you know that song?

If you're a sports fan you probably have to endure it all the time at live games over the public address.

When it comes to dog grooming salons, it's never a chant we want to hear. Or a joke we want to make.

The number one rule for every dog grooming salon: you must never, ever, let a dog escape.

So let's think about the doors in your salon for a minute. There is the front door. Outside the front door might be a car park. There might be a street with passing cars. Buses. Trucks.

Inside your premises, there is a separate door to the salon. And maybe there's a door out the back to a yard.

The door to your salon might be a Dutch door. That's a door that is cut in half. The bottom can be closed. The top half can swing open separately.

A Dutch door - provided the bottom section is high enough - is a practical solution. This is because you can keep the door closed. But still talk to the groomer in the salon. Or hand over a small dog into his or her arms. Without having to open the bottom half. Because at the other side of the door, you might have other dogs in the salon. At the first opportunity, they'll get to the other side.

And then it's just seconds away from the front door. Onto the car park. Or onto the street.

But this only happens if you let dogs run free in your salon. The potential for an escaping dog can be avoided completely. Put your dogs in a crate while they're waiting. Latch to an eye-hook in the wall. Or separate into holding cells.

If a dog escapes from your salon, you might not be able to retrieve him. The dog is lost. Trying to find its way home in a strange neighbourhood. Or the dog runs into the street. And gets struck by a passing motorist.

The dog was in your care. And you now have to explain to the owner that the dog is missing. Or it's been run over. This is such an avoidable tragedy.

The best solution is double doors. That is, two sets of doors separating the reception from the salon. It's also referred to as an air-lock space. There is room between the two doors. So you open one. Move into the air-lock space. Close the door. Then open the other one. Be vigilant about opening one door at a time when you're moving between the salon and reception.

The chances of a dog escaping should never be underestimated. You simply don't want to take the risk. So put in two sets of doors. Create an air-lock space.

Additionally, some dogs are clever enough to work out door handles. Dogs can often figure out that pressing down on a lever handle will give them the freedom they desperately need. If you have these, replace them with round door knobs. Or install the levers so that you have to pull up instead of push down to open. That'll confuse the little Houdini dogs in your care.

And another thing. Make sure to put a bold bright sign on your door that says something along the lines of 'Restricted Access, Employees Only, Open this Door at Pain of Death'.

Too many customers assume that it's okay for them to open doors willy-nilly. They have no appreciation for the risk of a dog escaping. Really, they don't. They live in their own little worlds. They simply don't understand.

This is the number one safety hazard for your business. For your career and your livelihood. Everything you've worked hard to achieve.

This may all sound a little bit OTT (over the top). But I know one thing. I never, ever want to have the conversation with a customer telling them that their dog escaped from my salon. Or worse.

85. Managing Collars & Leads

When a dog comes for a bath, it has to get naked. Which means removing the collar and lead.

You might already have a 'system' for managing collars and leads.

Maybe not.

And then what happens? The customer shows up to collect their dog. You start looking up and down the salon for the lead. The dog should already be wearing its collar. With a little bow attached to the D-ring.

You've got too many leads to choose from. You can't remember which lead belongs to which dog.

You grab three random leads. Hold them up to the customer. Your face scrunches up sheepishly and you ask 'was it the red one?'

Sound familiar?

From the customer's perspective, it doesn't look good. It's not professional. It makes you and your business look scattered. Sloppy.

Let's take a step back. You are proud of your grooming. You have done your best scissoring. The dog looks great. In your mind, you're already fast-forwarding to that little moment of joy. When the owner sees their freshly transformed companion. It's thrilling isn't it?

Not a lot of people get this kind of satisfaction in their jobs. Six or more times a day. But we do.

And then we blow it because we can't find the lead. It undermines the customer experience.

If you don't already have a system for managing collars and leads, try the following:

* purchase a bunch of those medium sized plastic hooks. The ones that are sticky on the back.
* stick the hooks to a wall. Or a door in your salon.
* get a little whiteboard and hang this above the hooks.
* draw some boxes on the whiteboard with permanent marker. Directly above each hook.
* when a dog arrives, hang the lead on the hook. Use an erasable marker to write the dog's name in the box above the hook.

It's a simple solution. Old school. But it does the trick. I still use this method today.

86. Smelly Shop, Smelly Shop

PRECIOUS: I cannot count the number of times I've walked into a dog grooming salon. And been assaulted by the horrible stench of pee and poo. I'm in the industry. Imagine what our customers think. Not pleasant.

Do you know why Starbucks is so successful? It's not because they sell coffee. It's because they sell an 'experience'. The experience is about walking into an atmosphere that looks warm and inviting. And smells wonderful. They were onto the 'smell' thing from the start. They wouldn't allow customers to smoke. The smell of smoke took away from the aroma of roasted coffee.

Upmarket pet boutiques don't like to 'smell' like a traditional pet shop. So, any pig's ears or pizzles are all wrapped in air-tight packaging. Instead of the whiff of air-dried pork, customers enjoy the light scent of lavender or citronella. Totally changes the 'experience'.

The same must apply to our salons. We sell our services with words like 'doggie spa'. Or 'luxurious blueberry muffin shampoos'. It conjures up an image of a semi-tropical retreat. Somewhere their dogs will be lovingly pampered.

When they walk through the door, does the expectation live up to the reality?

This is easy to fix. But it takes discipline and effort. Cleaning effort in particular.

There is a sense of order in how we apply our senses. First: what we smell. Second: what we see. Third: what we hear.

Put yourself in the shoes of the dog owner.

What are they smelling and seeing when they come to you?

Your sense of smell will be accustomed to the salon. So, step outside for a minute. Breathe some fresh air. Then walk into your salon as if you're coming in off the street. Can you smell anything? Is it a good smell? Or a bad smell?

It has to be a good smell. You're not selling 'dog grooming'. You are selling an 'experience'. Like Starbucks. The customer is willing to pay $5 for a cup of coffee. Instead of $1 at the greasy-spoon across the road.

Do you want to be greasy spoon? Or Starbucks?

Wash your towels often. At a high temperature. With good detergent. This will kill the bacteria. Don't just let them dry overnight on a rack. You want those towels fragrant. Not freaky.

Instead of cotton / fabric towels, use absorbent cloths. They still need to be washed regularly. But they don't hold the smell as much as fabric.

The floors in your salon need to be mopped thoroughly every day. You have a lot of doggy traffic coming through. Dogs will mark. They'll have accidents.

Ever notice that the number of accidents increases dramatically on a rainy day? That's because some owners get lazy exercising their dog before grooming. So they're quite happy to make it your problem.

So educate your customers. Ask them to exercise their dog before grooming. Not only have they had the chance to pee and poo. They will have burned off some energy. They'll be less exuberant, or more compliant. You can even offer the customer free poo bags if it helps get the message across.

Your bathtub and drainage also need special attention. Make sure the tub is sterilised thoroughly. Always keep the drainage clear so you don't get any of that nasty back-whiff sewer smell. A lot of dirt and hair and general gunk go down that drain. Take one of those long metal coils. Slide it up and down the drain. In and out. To break apart any build-up.

Take your rubbish out on a daily basis. Don't leave it in the salon. It is teeming with all kinds of bacteria and unpleasantness.

A friend of mine is hyper clean. I have never seen a salon that sparkles as brilliantly. It smells wonderful. She always has fresh lilies at the front. They have a strong fragrance. That smell of lilies is the customer's first experience. And then the customer sees her bright, clean, organised salon. Her iPod is connected to speakers. Playing English choral music. The atmosphere is, literally, divine. After all, cleanliness is next to godliness.

IV. Grooming Career

87. Self-Confidence

I get nauseous anytime I have to speak to an audience. Or run a workshop. My skin gets clammy. I'm sweating bucket loads. If you've been to one of my talks you may have noticed. The first few minutes are always a bit shaky. My hands grab the lectern so tightly my skin is white at the knuckles. My throat is constricted. I sound like Mickey Mouse. Which is not an appropriate voice for a guy of my, uhm, stature.

After a few minutes though, I will get into my stride. I will find my voice. Which is both gruff and smooth. Like somebody who should host a jazz show on the radio. The anxiety falls away. Now I'm starting to get interactive. Taking questions from the audience. Getting a few laughs.

When I first started grooming, I had a similar experience. I was apprehensive about taking the scissors to the dog's coat. Because once the hair is cut, it's cut. I would have all kinds of self-doubt. What if I cut at the wrong angle? What if I take too much off?

I was lucky though to have a great instructor. Gill East. She didn't molly-coddle me. But she understood. She took my fears. My hesitation. My over-analysis. She told me to stuff all these worries into an envelope. And push the envelope to one side. And to get on with grooming the dog.

'Just do it' she would say. Again and again. I'm sure one of our customers was an ad agency exec working for Nike. And that he overheard her shouting at me… Just Do It.

She also took me to the side once. She explained quietly, forcefully, that if I did something wrong, it was not the end of the world. No, really. It really was not the end of the world.

There are bigger things in life for people to get hysterical about than a disappointing haircut on their dog.

She reminded me of Mr. Miyagi in The Karate Kid. She insisted I cut and cut and cut. Like the Karate Kid washing cars and painting fences. All this experience of dog after dog after dog was creating muscle memory in my hands. After a while, I found myself grooming instinctively.

Then I started enjoying it. Because I could see that my hands, with a pair of scissors in them, were creating beautiful shapes. And this was so exciting. First, I was getting good. Then I was getting fast. Not 'fast' in a reckless kind of way. Just more efficient. I was learning to groom smarter.

This is how I overcame my worries and fears about my ability. Repetition. Repetition. Repetition.

And now with my speaking engagements: the more I do, the better I get.

So, if you are lacking confidence. Unsure about your ability to groom dogs. My simple advice is to keep grooming. Just Do It.

It takes a lot of discipline and mind control to stuff those worries into an envelope. But practise it. I don't allow my fears to cripple me.

I am not alone in being nervous. And I'm not embarrassed to admit it. If you find that the mental exercise of stuffing your worries into an envelope isn't working, then listen to other groomers. Perhaps your colleagues. Or online in a dog grooming forum. They too will admit they're nervous. And they might suggest other remedies that work for you.

Remember, I'm a self-described nervous wreck. I had to find a mechanism to manage my fears. And then I unlocked my inner groomer.

88. Finding a Good Instructor

I have now been teaching for many years. I enjoy watching students progress. And I like working with people. I'm a people-person. So I never take for granted the privilege I have being a teacher.

Naturally, when students are looking for a prospective instructor, they'll be looking for somebody with the right qualifications. Certifications. Awards. Just like signing up for any course, the instructor needs to have some form of certification. Something that identifies their expertise and authority.

I have these qualifications. But I can also back up my credentials with a cabinet full of trophies and rosettes (I am not saying this in a bragging, thump-my-chest kind of way).

There is no guarantee that awards and certificates make a good teacher though. Let's face it, when you win an award, you don't have to say very much, if anything at all. When you go for certification, you don't have to speak. When you go for your teaching certificate, it's not like you have to demonstrate how well you communicate and inspire.

If you're an aspiring groomer looking for an instructor, you need to make sure that the instructor at least has the right qualifications. That these are current. But the critical element is the instructor's ability to teach.

I have memories of favourite teachers at school. They knew their subject well. But what really made them stand out was their ability to inspire.

So, you need to be able to identify with your instructor, understand him or her. And your teacher has to take an interest in you personally for you to stay motivated through your course. So before you decide on a course with a certain instructor, make sure you get the chance to meet. Figure out whether or not this is somebody who 'speaks' to you. It will make all the difference in the world. Look for a good sense of humour. Look for empathy. Genuine interest in your ambition to become a groomer. What is the instructor's top priority? Making sure that your needs are met correctly? Or making sure you pay your course fees on time?

89. Training & Education

Certification and recognised qualifications are a good thing for groomers. It helps to establish standards. Not just in how a breed should be styled. But how we should work.

There are two parts to qualification. There is your 'Theory'. Which is your academic knowledge of dog grooming. And your 'Practical'. Which is your actual skill.

Getting qualified will test both of these. The organisation providing the qualification will differ, depending on where you live. In the UK for example, we have the City & Guilds qualification.

Employers will often look for a groomer with a qualification. It reassures them that the candidate has been trained to a certain standard. And has proved their competence to authorities in the industry.

I therefore recommend training with a view to getting qualified. But don't rush into your exams. Do your training. Get some experience. Take your tests when your instructor tells you you're ready.

You can, of course, be a very good groomer and have no qualification at all. If you have your own established business that might be fine. And your customers might be happy.

If they go to the hair-dresser they expect their stylist to have done some training. But they don't necessarily expect their hairdresser to hold a nationally recognised qualification.

Dog grooming is different though. And customers are increasingly aware of the need for qualification. It reassures them that their dog will be groomed according to breed standards. And that the grooming will be carried out professionally. With all the right health and safety considerations.

If you're a qualified groomer therefore, it's worth advertising this on your website or shop window.

In addition to how much you'll learn from getting your qualification, there is 'continuing education'. And in the UK we are getting better at this by the day. I am asked more and more to speak at workshops. Provide demonstrations.

Going to workshops is great fun. Not just for me. You get to focus on a particular subject – like Creative Colouring. Or hand-stripping. Poodle cuts. And more.

Seeing how other people do things will improve our grooming. We'll learn ways to groom more efficiently. We'll learn tricks and tips from masters at their craft. Plus it keeps our grooming fresh. The science and art of dog grooming is constantly evolving. When we go to workshops, we learn these things. And we can bring them into our own grooming.

Additionally, it helps us feel like we belong to a community of dog groomers. That there are others like us, facing many of the same challenges. At workshops, we meet these people. We make friends. Contacts. We network. These people are only a phone call or an email or a Tweet away from being able to get advice. Hear about new products. Events. Gossip.

I totally encourage your continuing education. And I look forward to seeing you at my next workshop.

90. Becoming an Instructor / Training Centre

Have you noticed in the last few years the number of independent salons that are now advertising dog grooming courses? The salon owner has built up their business. They can rely on a steady flow of dogs. Either they or their groomer or assistant have to groom the dogs. So why not take on a paying student? Have them help out with the grooming. Teach them how to groom. Make money.

Back this up with a little bit of paperwork. And the salon owner is now taking in more money each month. As a business model, brilliant.

But it comes with enormous responsibility.

If you set yourself up for taking on students you need to back this up with authentic good quality teaching. Plus all the other requirements. Like insurance. Proper Health and Safety Awareness.

Otherwise you put your reputation at risk. Not just from unhappy students. But unhappy customers.

Your regular customers come to you because they are pleased with the standard of grooming that you provide. But once you put students onto those dogs, there is a chance of accidents. And incorrect grooming. You risk losing those customers. Especially the ones who don't like to see somebody new grooming their dog each time they come in.

That said, it is perfectly legitimate, at a certain point in your career, to think about sharing your skills with students. And earning the additional money that can come from dog grooming courses (which are not cheap).

And besides, teaching has to take place in all professions. Otherwise, how do the next generation learn? Whether it's your hairdressers. Or the plumber. The baker. Even in hospitals. Young residents, fresh out of medical college, develop their skills under the supervision of an attending physician.

But is it right for you to turn your salon into a training centre? And turn yourself from groomer to instructor?

Here are a few questions to ask before deciding to become an instructor:

1. am I a people person? Am I a good communicator? A lot of us go into grooming, as we like to say, because we don't have to deal with people. Guess what. We have to deal with people. Whether these are customers or colleagues. But if you feel you're not a people person, then maybe teaching isn't for you. On the other hand, if you can tell a good joke down the pub. And you know how to make people feel at ease, then maybe you are a natural-born teacher.

2. do I have enough patience to watch somebody make a mistake? Even after I have shown them six times how to do the same thing? If you're a parent who has enjoyed raising your children, then this might be a no-brainer. Teaching could be your calling.

3. do I really care that this person learns something from me? Am I just into this for the money? You might take on a couple of students and sure, you might like the extra money. But you'll also see how much it can take out of you if your heart really isn't in it. If you enjoy the thrill of passing on knowledge. And seeing people learn and improve. Plus it helps to pay the bills. Then yes, teaching could be the right thing to do.

4. do I have the adequate skills and qualifications, and have I 'mastered' my craft well enough? Do I really have the authority and legitimacy to train others? Have I really seen enough and dealt with so many situations? If the student surprises me with a stupid move, will I know instinctively how to react? If you're good on your feet in a situation, then teaching could be right for you.

5. are there perhaps other ways of making additional revenue in my business without having to provide dog grooming courses? If you run a business, there are always opportunities for making extra money. Yes, teaching is one of them. But it's all-consuming. Challenge yourself to think about other opportunities that might be easier and less demanding than teaching. Maybe you like acting? Set up a camera. Record a video of yourself grooming a designer breed. If it's a good video, maybe you can sell it.

The dog grooming industry needs good teachers. But be careful what you are getting yourself into. Teaching is enormously rewarding. I personally love it. Ask yourself the questions above. You have to decide if your salon will continue to operate just as a salon. Or as a teaching establishment. It will make a difference to your existing clientele.

After you've asked yourself the questions above. And you believe even more that it's the right thing to do. For you and your business. Then you have my total support. It's exciting and rewarding.

91. Old Masters vs the New

There is often rivalry between an Old Master and a young apprentice. If you're an experienced dog groomer or run your own salon, you might be that Old Master. You might have honed your craft over the years. Won all kinds of distinctions. These have given you a certain confidence. You have earned 'tenure' in the business. Which basically means you get away with saying whatever you want. You have happy customers. A wall full of ribbons and awards and trophies. Maybe even pictures of yourself with the President. Maybe a Queen.

Along comes somebody less experienced than you. Perhaps the very assistant or groomer you've hired. And here you are working alongside them. In your salon. You observe the way they groom. It's different. You might not like it. You might be annoyed.

While dog grooming is increasingly standardised (this is a good thing) and similar techniques used on most breeds, it still remains a craft. It is creative. Organic.

Some people take their talent and use it in different ways from us. You might not like how they get from point A to point B. But you can't fault the result.

It happens to me. I get so stuck in my teaching ways. I am so accustomed to correcting a student, I forget that, hey, actually, they might have something. A certain technique. Style. Or trick that I can learn from. And that's really aggravating. In an emotionally threatening kind of way (not really, I'm just saying that for dramatic effect).

To be fair, this doesn't really happen with a student who is just starting out. But I see it sometimes with a student who already has some experience. They will have a way of working that jars against the way I normally work. My impulse is to correct it.

But then I remind myself. No, let's give it a minute. Let's see where this is heading. Provided it's not a dramatic departure from the breed standard. Or the owner's expectations. And often I am surprised. In a nice way. Because the student achieves a certain result I didn't originally anticipate.

From one Old Master to another, this is my advice. Keep an open mind. Don't get stuck in your own way of doing things. Don't be intimidated by changing routines or processes or techniques. Dog grooming, like all trades or crafts or professions, continues to evolve.

I know a lot of groomers of my generation who still don't own a trimmer or a blaster. I know of groomers who will blend using thinning shears. A snap-on comb will achieve the same results in seconds. Saving lots of time.

I encourage you to embrace the new to stay current. And who knows, it may result in your own grooming improving a notch or two. So that even you, God's Great Gift to Grooming, will be able to groom an extra dog per day. Or improve your own finishes. And that helps your business.

Remind yourself of what attracted you to this business in the first place. It probably wasn't just to bathe and brush short-coated breeds. Dog grooming is still an art form. There will always come along those upstarts who can teach an old Master. Something to make grooming easier. Perhaps faster. Possibly even more fun. While still making the dog look like a million bucks.

92. Burn-Out: I Hate My Job

There are times when we're down. Hate what we do. We work too hard. We don't get the recognition we deserve. Our customers don't appreciate us. This sort of thing happens to most people in most trades or businesses. It's a life thing.

When people talk to me about it, I usually discover that they are working too hard. They've gone too long without a break. A decent holiday. They run their own salon. They can't possibly let down their customers.

But our customers get to go on holiday, right?

If you happen to be away when they need grooming, they will wait for you to get back. Maybe they'll go for a one-time groom elsewhere. Provided you have a good rapport with them. And they like what you do – why would they be regular customers if they didn't – they will come back.

I will say this slowly now so you understand: it's okay. You may take a holiday.

But like everybody who plans a holiday – bankers, teachers, politicians, bakers or builders - you have to let other people know. In your case, tell your regular customers. And then work out their next appointment around the dates you are away.

Trust me, we all need to take a break. We need to step back from the day-in day-out grind. Otherwise we will burn out. Get bored. Frustrated. Unhappy.

Yet here we are with a skill. A trade. A profession which means we get to be our own boss. Or have the potential to become our own boss.

If you're too busy to take a holiday, you're too busy. Nice problem to have. Stop allowing yourself to let your customers run you into the ground. You have to protect yourself. For the sake of your future. The longevity of your career.

There are a couple of strategies. It might be time to raise your prices. Sure, you'll lose a few customers. But you'll make it up with the price increase. And, in fact, with the psychology of pricing, you may attract more customers than you lose. Funny how that works, but it's true.

If you are open six days a week, consider going down to five days. It's not unusual for a grooming salon to be closed on a Monday. So, you work Tuesday through Saturday.

Another option is to consider hiring a bather or assistant to take some of the pressure off you.

If you have taken all these steps and you're still not convinced, then consider additional training. Workshops. Perhaps a seminar. A Master Class. Or a dog grooming show. These are great for having a moan with other groomers. But also for gaining some perspective on your own situation. Reminding yourself how good you've really got it.

You'll also get some fresh ideas that you may want to try out. There is a lot of creative stuff happening. Especially in the all-natural, holistic area. Treatments like the Blueberry and Vanilla facial. Or have you tried out the Dead Sea Mud bath? These are just a couple of examples. But it points out that dog grooming is still dynamic. Progressive. Exciting. Trying these out may just give you the boost you need.

93. Why Compete

PRECIOUS: Colin is a bag of hammers when it comes to competing. Ask him about an upcoming contest and his face does that nervous twitching sneezing thing.

I love competing. LOVE it. But I know it's not for everybody. You're in a big room. Other groomers eyeing you suspiciously. Judges in suits. Looking serious and important. Somebody holding a stopwatch. No wonder Colin morphs into a Zombie.

But I have good news. You can compete without being competitive. Let me explain. Competing, and preparing for competition is great. It develops our time-keeping. Improves our skills.

So go into competition for your own sake. Instead of getting rattled by the prospect of losing. Or getting wound up by the prospect of winning. The prize money. The new car. The all-expenses paid holiday.

Do it for the development of your skills. For learning new tricks. Working more efficiently.

You'll get to meet other groomers. Which is always a nice thing.

You'll meet suppliers. Be introduced to exciting new products. Develop relationships with them. Put a face to a name. Network.

Plus it can be great fun. Competition helps to break up our routine. It keeps us engaged in the industry. And the more people who participate, the more buzz it creates.

94. Preparing For Competition

PRECIOUS: When Colin was competing, he'd buy a wall calendar. Post it in the salon. Circle the competition dates in red felt marker. Then put an X across every day we got closer to the date.

He'd be the first to send his entry forms. He'd call the event organisers to confirm they had received his application. He'd call them a week later to double-check.

If he didn't already have a dog in mind, he'd go into this really strange mood. He'd be scoping every dog that came into the salon. When he spotted a potential candidate – a good specimen – he'd elbow his way to reception. He needed to groom this dog.

He could see immediately if the dog would make a good specimen. But he needed to know if the dog would be easy to handle.

So he'd take the dog to the table. Often, the dog would be too fidgety. Or restless. Colin would be disappointed. He'd have to find another dog.

Eventually, he'd come up with one. He'd make the arrangements with the customer. Usually a free grooming once a week. The customers were always happy to participate. They didn't have to pay for the grooming. And their little dog was going to be treated like a celebrity.

Over the next six or eight weeks, Colin would practise and practise. He'd take pictures of his finished cut. Then he would make tweaks the following week. Until he mastered the cut that he was after. The cut that he wanted to replicate in the contest ring.

He'd print off a picture. Post it on the salon wall. In the bathroom. At home. I would watch him study that picture. Again and again.

He also kept a secret list. Which I found one day. And kept. It's his 'requirements' for the perfect dog. It's what he looks for in a dog for competition. On the top he had scribbled 'Confidential'. This is what it looked like:

CONFIDENTIAL

The Perfect Dog:

- Will be a good breed standard. Unless mixed.
- Will have patience on the grooming table.
- Will be of the correct weight.
- Will have a healthy coat.
- Will be easy to handle. We must have a good rapport.
- X-Factor. The dog must have winning appeal. Even before it's had the haircut.

I'm sure Colin won't mind my sharing his secret list with you. He used to be a lot more obsessive about these things. But now he just wants to share everything. Except his scissors. But I understand.

95. International Competition & Your Dog

Competitive dog groomers will travel thousands of miles around the world to compete. I've done it during my time with Groom Team USA and Groom Team Scotland. It's a big investment on our part. Not only in terms of money. But time. Effort. Jet lag. And those tiny cramped seats in an airplane.

When we travel abroad to compete, we don't take our own dogs with us. So we have to rent a dog. All of this gets arranged beforehand. The dog is rented from other groomers. Or the show producers. And often involves the exchange of money. As a competitive groomer, I would have to pay a lot for this. For the privilege of grooming somebody else's dog.

Plus there are tight time constraints. Competitors sometimes don't actually see their dog until just minutes before entering the ring.

It can get a bit stressful.

And it can really be stressful if the dog you are renting is in a bad state. I have seen a dog infested with parasites. I have seen a dog with its coat covered in urine stains given to a competitor. At this point, you can't really say no. Because you don't really have any choice.

Is this deliberate sabotage? Greediness? Lack of care for the dog? Don't get me wrong. I've only seen this happen a few times. For the most part, when I was competing, I was able to rent excellent specimens.

There are steps you can take to prevent this from happening to you.

First, be sure to see pictures of the dog via email. Make sure that this is actually the dog you will be given to compete with. You may want to pay a little more to the person renting you the dog if they agree to keep the dog's coat in a good condition.

Also ask if the dog is experienced in the competition ring. You don't want to compete with a dog that hasn't been socialised. Or is so unaccustomed to competition. You'll lose valuable time and effort just on the handling.

Ask the person renting the dog if they would compete with that dog. Personally, I would never rent a dog that I myself wouldn't compete with.

If at all possible, try to spend time with the dog the day before the competition. So you have an opportunity for some bonding. This will help ensure a smoother time once you are both in the competition ring.

If you have been fortunate to have a good specimen and you do not place, don't blame the dog. It wasn't your day. And there will always be other competitions.

96. In the Contest Ring

Remember when we talked about Method Grooming. Now, you need to be a Method Competitor.

It's the day of. You've done all your practising. Your fingers are twitching. You're eager to perform that final perfect cut.

Everything is in place.

You've arrived at the competition site early.

All your tools have been sharpened.

You have the perfect comb.

You've slept well.

You're hydrated. But not too hydrated.

You're wearing comfortable shoes.

A smart, clean tabard.

Your lucky charm. Don't forget your lucky charm.

Let's imagine it's an hour before the competition starts. If you have somebody travelling with you, ask them to look after your dog for twenty minutes.

Take a walk outside. Find a patch of nature to walk through. Or the far end of the car park. Breathe some fresh air.

De-clutter your brain.

Then, take a few minutes to rehearse. Think about securing your dog to the table. How you'll lay your tools out.

Repeat your 'method' to yourself.

Make your way back to the competition hall. Take a pee break. Breathe. It's time to get into the 'zone'.

You are now at your table. Your dog is secured. Your tools are laid out for maximum efficiency. Make sure you've only laid out the tools you'll need.

The Master of Ceremonies makes the announcement. You may begin.

You're in the zone. The only object you see is your dog on the table. Don't get distracted by the other groomers and their dogs. Or the judges who may start walking past to watch you in action. Or the spectators who may be excited and noisy.

Concentrate fully and completely on your dog. Your time. Your Method.

What's your Method?

Let's look at an example. You have a Miniature Poodle. You have a time limit of 90 minutes.

Clip the feet, face and tail. Ten minutes.
Block the dog in a rough shape. Twenty minutes.

That's thirty minutes gone. You have sixty minutes to complete your finish, balance and profile.

Follow your Method. Back. Front. Body. Head. Tail.

You may be grooming automatically. The muscle memory from your practise sessions has taken over.

Some contests will give you two hours. That extra thirty minutes will make all the difference. But it can also make you over-scissor. Over-correct. Leaving more room for error.

Work toward the finished image of your dog.
Don't make any stylistic departures.
Keep an ear out for the MC's time-checks.
Make sure you are hitting each milestone of your method. Just as you've done in your practise sessions.

Then scissor comfortably and confidently to your finish. Perfecting your dog so that it matches the picture you stuck to the bathroom mirror at home.

You're done. The MC has called Time.

97. The Judges are Coming

So the Master of Ceremonies has called Time. This is it. The moment of truth. Clear your table. Stand your dog. Preferably on material that compliments what you're wearing. But offsets the colour of the dog. For example, if you have a black dog, do not wear a black tabard. Or stand your dog on black material.

You also need to know how to 'stack' your dog. This means presenting the dog to the show judges. But you have to make sure you are stacking correctly for the breed. So make sure you've done your research on this.

Don't get too eager about stacking your dog immediately. You only need to stack when the judges come to you. Save the dog's strength for the moment of reckoning. Which is NOW.

As the judges approach, stack your dog. Look confidently – and pleasantly - into their eyes. Let them know you have done your best. In their eyes, you have.

They will circle around your dog. Inspecting. They'll stand back. Take a look. One of them may ask for your comb. Or make a funny gesture with the hand. Make sure you give the judge the comb you've been using. This is important. A different comb will lift or fluff the hair differently.

When the judge takes your comb, hold the tips of the dog's nose and tail. As the judge is moving around your dog, make sure you are likewise moving. Give the judge the best possible access. Don't get in the way. Let her - or him - focus without distraction.

During the judging, stay alert to what the judge is doing. She may ask you a question. Provide short, simple and truthful answers. Do not start a narrative. Or talk about the challenges of the coat. Or how you are personally feeling. Or how awful the weather and the traffic have been. Just be delightful. Proud. To the point.

The judge has completed her assessment. She is ready to move onto the next competitor. She will hand your comb back to you. Take it. And make sure your dog remains correctly stacked for the judge's final look.

Now allow your dog to rest. But keep an eye out for the judges' progress through the other competitors. They may suddenly re-visit you.

This is also a good time to offer your dog some water.

A judge may spend two minutes with you but then five minutes on another dog. Don't let this bother you. All judges work in different ways.

Okay, so now the judges have gone over all the dogs. They are doing their final circuit. This is time again to showcase your brilliant work of art. If undecided they may come back to you a second time.

98. Judging

Generally, judges at dog shows like Crufts or Westminster are not comparing one dog to another. They are comparing a dog to an ideal specimen. That ideal exists in their mind. Which is determined by the guidance given in a kennel club's breed standards.

Likewise, judges at grooming competitions aren't necessarily comparing your finish to that of the other competitors. They, too, will have an image in mind of a good finish on the breed they are judging. It's not you versus the groomer at the next table. It's your finish versus an ideal. Your score represents how closely you got to that ideal.

At least, that's how I judge. Or how I think judging should take place. It helps me to keep the judging objective.

Of course, judging requires some subjectivity. Some allowance for the dog's natural structure. One Cockerpoo might have a wildly different shape from another. The coat textures will vary. So I take these things into account.

A good judge will intuit the so-called 'best cut' for the dog. They can do it automatically. With that 'best cut' in mind, the judge will assess the scissoring skills. The balance. The overall finish.

At the end of a class I have to select three groomers. The winners will love me for selecting them. But I have empathy for those I didn't select. Will they respect my decision? Will they resent me? Maybe even hate me?

I'm sensitive to these things. So when I choose a winner, I have to be confident in my selection. My decision has to be made with that objectivity.

I make it a priority therefore to stay on top of my own education. And I only judge classes I feel confidently about the breeds being styled.

I admit I don't feel strongest judging classes like sporting (gun) dogs. Or hand-stripping. It's not because I can't achieve the grooming myself. These are simply not my areas of expertise. When I judge, I'll talk to the competitors. I'll provide a critique. And feedback. So I stick to what I know best.

When I organise a competition, I get the best possible judges in their categories. The ones I know to be strong in a particular class. The judges I trust to make their selections objectively. And I look for that skill. That ability to intuit the 'best cut' for the dog they are judging.

99. Sportsmanship

PRECIOUS: I have said before, you don't need to be competitive to compete. That's true. To a certain point.

But there comes a tipping point when you've done your time. You've practised like crazy. You've done all the right things. You've competed before. You've won things here and there. You know the circuit. You know the judges. You know the other competitors. You've made incredible sacrifices. And you believe, to the pit of your stomach, it's your turn to really WIN. To be crowned champion.

The prize might be something you really really want. Like a wonderful handbag. Cash that will help you buy that new set of scissors. Or take that holiday.

Winning first place will give you recognition by your peers. By the industry. You can truly describe your own business as 'award-winning'. And put the trophy and the ribbons and the pictures on your 'hero wall' in your salon so that your adoring customers will know their dog is being groomed by the best.

Yes, the knock-on effect of a little bit of celebrity. Perhaps an article in your local newspaper or magazine. Or even coverage in a national industry magazine or website. Quotes from your parents about how proud they are. A kind comment from an old neighbour who always knew you'd go far.

The stakes are getting high when you dream about how much this will turn your business and your life around. Soon you'll be invited to provide workshops and master classes by other salons up and down the country. Yep. You're starting to get competitive. And no matter what field you are in, whether you are a Chess Master or a dancer or a cyclist, real winners are singularly occupied with winning. Not winning isn't an option.

What's more important than winning though, is 'sportsmanship'. Or should that be 'sportspersonship'? We're usually good at this in the early days of competing. Because we're new to it. We don't really expect to win until we've earned our spurs.

But now, we've got the guts. So where's the Glory?

We are, at this stage, at risk of getting above ourselves. We might truly believe it's our turn for that coveted trophy. For prize money. And what happens if we don't win?

We storm out of the ring. Waving our arms about like a wrongly convicted mafioso. Snarling with anger and outrage. We create a DRAMA.

We might even scream at the judges. Raging at them that they should have gone to Specsavers (the opticians). We curse our fellow competitors. Wishing them the eternal damnation of fire and brimstone.

And then we blame our dogs.

We assume it's fixed.

We despair at the world of dog grooming. And swear to take up a new profession. Like becoming an accountant in Slough. Working in an office as far away from grooming as possible.

We take out our anger and despair, frustration and conspiracy theories on everyone. Except ourselves.

Okay. So maybe I've layered it a bit thick here. I'm doing that for dramatic effect. Especially the Slough bit.

When competing, we have to remember there are a whole bunch of factors at work and there is no possible way that we can control an outcome.

First, there's your dog and whether or not it's a good specimen plus your ability to groom it well according to breed standards.

Then there are the judges, each with his or her own bias or idiosyncrasy that you can't possibly control or predict.

On top of that, there's the other competitors. They might have done the hard yards just as you've done. Maybe even more so. Perhaps they have a tiny bit of finesse that is a touch superior to yours.

And it may be that you just didn't get 100 per cent fully into 'the zone'. Maybe you're too focused on winning, the tension undermines your natural talent to finish the dog as well as you've done in your practise sessions.

When you get too wound up, you don't allow yourself the freedom for a bit of creative flair in your dog grooming.

So my advice is that if you find yourself horribly aggrieved that things haven't gone your way, count to ten and repeat the word 'sportsmanship' to yourself. Always stay professional. Look, there will be other competitions. Today just wasn't your day. For whatever reason. But whatever you do, don't make a scene. You need to play the long game here. And the last thing you want is to come across looking like a sore loser. The dog grooming circuit is a small world. Always stay cool. And instead of creating a reputation as a hysterical diva, build yourself a reputation as a worthy competitor and consummate professional.

100. Placing in a Competition

PRECIOUS: The judges have made a decision. They've called YOUR name. It may take a few seconds for this to sink in. You might not believe it. Wow. You've done it. Yay!

Typical Colin though, he always feels guilty for winning. He feels badly for the ones who didn't win. He can't help it like that. He's glad to win. But I always see him give this apologetic look to the other competitors.

Which is very English of him. Shying away from the limelight like that.

Despite this, he still has to observe the 'protocol'. By this, I mean what he has to do when he's been selected.

It's perfectly understandable to be overcome with joy and emotion. You might collapse in disbelief. Or sheer exhaustion. It's the realisation of everything you've worked so hard to achieve.

You might also give a great big whoop of delight. Or surprise. You can't control yourself. You fling your arms around the judge. Give them a great big kiss.

It could be crazy and impulsive. There's no controlling how you might react.

To this, I say, give yourself over to the moment. For a minute. Feel the joy. Feel the accomplishment.

But make sure you secure your dog first. Then acknowledge the judges. Show them the respect for making the right decision. A handshake. A big thank you. With a smile.

Then acknowledge your competitors. They might already be taking their dogs off the table. Putting their things away. Be gracious in your victory. Shake their hands. Take a moment to thank them for making it a tough contest.

Never, ever, be smug. You will have won a lot of fans with your victory. People will cheer from the sidelines for you. They'll be happy for you. Thank them with a wave and a smile. Or a clenched fist that says 'yippee – I won!'

Then come the awards. This might happen immediately after the class. Or at the end of the day.

The MC or event officials will steer you in the right direction.

The class winners may be asked to take their places at a podium. Certificates or trophies or medals will be presented. Photos will be taken. Take your dog with you. And your comb. Make sure to stack correctly for the photo-op. Enjoy the moment.

If you placed first in your class, you'll be asked to stay on, for example, for 'Best in Show' or 'Groomer of the Year'. It depends on the competition.

The winners of each class again need to present their dogs to the judges.

Follow all normal procedures as before. Be confident. Be courteous. Stack your dog. Have your comb ready.

The judges will circle round. Inspecting closely. They may confer. They may just submit their scores to the MC or event official.

There will be a few tense moments while you wait for the result. The winners will be announced.

Again, the same rush of excitement. If you win, indulge the moment. Acknowledge the judges' decision. Congratulate your competitors. Acknowledge the cheers from the audience.

Then take your place on the podium and collect your prize. Congratulations!

101. Be Proud

PRECIOUS: Colin is a humble guy. He doesn't like to show off. It's because he has these little demons of self-doubt. This built-in tendency to downplay his accomplishments.

He's got all these awards. But he doesn't trumpet them. He doesn't put them on display.

I had to wrench him by the arm to create his own little 'hero wall' in the salon. So now they're on show. Press cuttings. Medals. Ribbons. Trophies.

Before that, they collected dust. In some damp, neglected corner of his apartment.

When we were putting together his Academy website, we needed pictures to put online. Could Colin find any? It took weeks for him to dig these out. Forgotten in an old album. Turning yellow with age. They could have disintegrated. Crumbled into a million tiny pieces.

There is a Biblical expression. Don't hide your light under a bushel. Let it shine.

If you've placed in a competition. Won an award. Been presented with a ribbon. Or a trophy. Put it on your hero wall.

The same applies for your certificates. The qualifications you've earned.

Showcase them. Put them on display. Stand next to them. Fold your arms in triumph. Lift your head with pride. Take a big smile for the camera. You've earned it. Let the world know.

COLIN: Thank you, Precious. My little Ultra-Ego. Yes, Precious is the part of me that confronts those little demons. That makes me shake them out. She challenges my worry that others might think I'm showing off.

But I've had a chance to reflect on these accomplishments. I came to a realisation.

It could look like I'm showing off. But it's not. Because it's not about me. Not entirely.

I have three reasons for saying this.

First, a lot of money, effort and organisation go into holding a competition. A venue needs to be hired. Event managers need to be paid. Judges recruited. People travel great distances. A lot of volunteers give willingly of their time to make it happen. And the dogs patiently endure getting groomed. Again and again.

This is our chosen industry. We are privileged to be dog groomers. To keep our industry alive and exciting, we need to be progressive. So we have competitions. It raises the standards. It keeps things fresh. It keeps us engaged in true craftsmanship. It pushes the science. The development of new techniques. Tools. Products. Treatments.

This helps all groomers everywhere. And the biggest beneficiary of these innovations and improvements? Our dogs.

You could be cynical. You could say it's all about corporate sponsors trying to sell us stuff. Making money for anonymous shareholders.

I prefer to see the bright side. I see the excitement of everybody participating. The moments of pride and enthusiasm when a daughter, son, brother, sister gives their dog an amazing haircut. And the judges look on approvingly.

So, now, when I hang that great big ribbon on my hero wall, it shows I'm a part of this industry. I'm helping to maintain the excitement about this business. The little girl or boy who dreams of working with dogs will see my awards. This can inspire them. And create the next generation of dog groomers who will see this career as a privilege.

Second, my family, friends, colleagues and others. None of us is an island. We have people – and dogs - in our lives who have helped us. The mother or father who presented us with a puppy in the happy days of our childhood. The older sister or brother. Who drove us to countless dog shows and competitions. The person at Church or School. Who let us practise our scissoring on their Cocker Spaniel. The person who gave us our first job. The customers who come into our salon. Who trust us with their dogs. And, of course, the dogs themselves. Who put up with the constant bathing and brushing. Drying and combing. Clipping and scissoring.

We owe it to them. Because our victory - our award - doesn't belong singularly to us. It belongs to all of them. All those who helped us along the way.

To hang that ribbon up. Or spit polish that little gold medal. That silver cup. The trophy. This is, in part, their achievement. You owe it to them, therefore. I owe it to them. To acknowledge their contribution to our success.

Third, winning awards is good for business. Chances are you are not alone in your business. You may have a partner who is both financially and emotionally invested. You may have staff. They depend on a regular pay-check.

When you display your awards and certificates, you reassure your customers that you are an award-winning groomer. This carries prestige. It enhances your brand and reputation. It attracts new customers who want the best for their dog.

You might generate some local media interest. This increases awareness of your services.

All these things can bring you extra money. And with that, comes additional opportunities. You can buy that new bath. Take that much-needed holiday. Hire an assistant. Improve your lifestyle. Grow your business.

It doesn't happen overnight of course. You've worked hard. You've earned the accolades. Along with some financial advantages, you can be satisfied by the approval of your peers. And that's a nice warm fuzzy feeling you can't put a price on.

The End